Lonely planet

P9-CLC-148

Pocket
SINGAPORE
TOP SIGHTS · LOCAL LIFE · MADE EASY

Cristian Bonetto

In This Book

QuickStart Guide

Your keys to understanding the city – we help you decide what to do and how to do it

Need to Know
Tips for a smooth trip

Neighbourhoods
What's where

Explore Singapore

The best things to see and do, neighbourhood by neighbourhood

Top Sights
Make the most of your visit

Local Life
The insider's city

The Best of Singapore

The city's highlights in handy lists to help you plan

Best Walks
See the city on foot

Singapore's Best...
The best experiences

Survival Guide

Tips and tricks for a seamless, hassle-free city experience

Getting Around
Travel like a local

Essential Information
Including where to stay

Our selection of the city's best places to eat, drink and experience:

◎ **Sights**

✖ **Eating**

🍷 **Drinking**

⭐ **Entertainment**

🛍 **Shopping**

These symbols give you the vital information for each listing:

📞 Telephone Numbers	👶 Family-Friendly
🕑 Opening Hours	🐾 Pet-Friendly
P Parking	🚌 Bus
🚭 Nonsmoking	⛴ Ferry
@ Internet Access	M Metro/MRT
📶 Wi-Fi Access	🚋 Tram
🥗 Vegetarian Selection	🚆 Train
📖 English-Language Menu	

Find each listing quickly on maps for each neighbourhood:

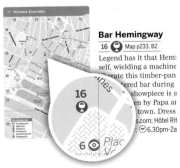

Bar Hemingway

16 🍷 Map p233, B2

Legend has it that Hemi self, wielding a machine rate this timber-pan ered bar during showpiece is a en by Papa ar town. Dress s.com; Hôtel Rit ⏰6.30pm-2a

Lonely Planet's Singapore

Lonely Planet Pocket Guides are designed to get you straight to the heart of the city.

Inside you'll find all the must-see sights, plus tips to make your visit to each one really memorable. We've split the city into easy-to-navigate neighbourhoods and provided clear maps so you'll find your way around with ease. Our expert authors have searched out the best of the city: walks, food, nightlife and shopping, to name a few. Because you want to explore, our 'Local Life' pages will take you to some of the most exciting areas to experience the real Singapore.

And of course you'll find all the practical tips you need for a smooth trip: itineraries for short visits, how to get around, and how much to tip the guy who serves you a drink at the end of a long day's exploration.

It's your guarantee of a really great experience.

Our Promise

You can trust our travel information because Lonely Planet authors visit the places we write about, each and every edition. We never accept freebies for positive coverage, so you can rely on us to tell it like it is.

QuickStart Guide 7

Explore Singapore 21

Worth a Trip:

QuickStart Guide

Welcome to Singapore

Smart, sharp and just a little sexy, Singapore is Southeast Asia's new 'It kid', subverting staid old stereotypes with ambitious architecture, dynamic museums, celebrity chefs and hip boutiques. Spike it with smoky temples, gut-rumble-inducing food markets and pockets of steamy jungle, and you might find that Asia's former wallflower is a much more intriguing bloom than you gave it credit for.

Merlion, Marina Bay
GAVIN HELLIER/GETTY IMAGES ©

Singapore
Top Sights

Gardens by the Bay (p28)

Singapore's latest buzz-inducing asset is a $1 billion 'super park' that makes horticulture hot. Explore its futuristic bio-domes and Supertrees, traverse its panoramic Skyway, and keep an eye out for Marc Quinn's floating infant.

Singapore Zoo (p122)

Singapore Zoo is one of the world's most inviting, enlightened animal sanctuaries, and a family-friendly must. Breakfast with orang-utans, sneak up to sleepy sloths and purr over rare white tigers.

Singapore Botanic Gardens (p128)

Singapore's Garden of Eden is the perfect antidote to the city's rat-race tendencies. Obscenely lush and verdant, its 74 hectares are home to rare orchids, a swan-studded lake and a romantic, ginger-centric restaurant.

Night Safari (p124)

Get up close and personal with a different kind of nightlife at this award-winning wildlife park, filled with an intriguing cast of free-roaming and free-flying creatures, great and small.

ANUP SHAH/GETTY IMAGES ©

National Museum of Singapore (p24)

Evocative, interactive exhibitions and striking old-meets-new architecture define Singapore's showcase museum. If you're after a gripping crash course in Singaporean history and culture, put this on your hit list.

SENG CHYE TEO/GETTY IMAGES ©

Universal Studios (p114)

Home to the planet's tallest duelling roller coasters, Universal Studios cranks up the adrenalin with seven themed areas pimped with enough rides, razzle-dazzle spectaculars and movie-set kitsch to thrill the most hardened of inner children.

UNIVERSAL STUDIOS SINGAPORE, RESORTS WORLD SENTOSA ©

Asian Civilisations Museum (p26)

Travel east to west across Asia at this engrossing ode to the continent's tapestry of cultures and traditions. It's like a glittering cultural attic, filled with ancient pottery and sculptures, mystical weaponry and dazzling jewels.

Southern Ridges (p140)

Monkey-peppered jungle, sculptural forest walkways and arresting views over city and sea – this multipark trail offers one of Singapore's most beautiful and accessible natural getaways.

Chinatown Heritage Centre (p66)

Immerse yourself in the struggles, scandals and hard-core grit of Chinatown's roller-coaster past at this unsung museum. You'll find it on a lantern-festooned street once better known for opium dens and coolie traders.

Singapore Local Life

Insider tips to help you find the real city

Once you've checked off the major sights, dig a little deeper and discover a more intimate side to the city – the side the locals know.

Chinatown Tastebuds & Temples (p68)

▶ Authentic hawker centres
▶ Hotspot bars and restaurants

The opium dens may have gone, but Chinatown's stubborn spirit kicks on with its in-yer-face market stalls, congee-slurping uncles and dragon-littered temples. Whether plonked on a plastic *kopitiam* (coffee-shop) stool or offering incense to the divine, prepare to savour enticing Chinatown.

Tiong Bahru (p62)

▶ Hip shops and cafes
▶ Heritage architecture

Not only famous for its art deco and mid-20th-century domestic architecture, this low-rise, laid-back neighbourhood is pulling in the trend-setters and hipsters with its ever-expanding booty of clued-in cafes, trendy bars and restaurants, and quirky shops, not to mention its top-notch bookstores.

A Stroll in Little India (p94)

▶ Mosques and temples
▶ Street life

A riot of colours, scents and evening crowds, Little India bursts with pungent pavement stalls, authentic Indian grub and sari-peddling shops blaring Indian pop. Hunt down market spices, pimp your skin with henna, and feast your eyes on a whimsical, fairy-tale mosque.

Katong (p86)

▶ Peranakan heritage
▶ Restaurants

Multicoloured heritage shophouses, restaurant-filled streets and shops peddling traditional ceramics, shoes and textiles. Katong is the heart and soul of Singapore's Peranakan culture. At its southern end is cycle-friendly East Coast Park, dotted with seafood restaurants and bars facing a boat-laden sea.

Geylang (p88)

▶ Street food
▶ Nightlife

Gateway between heaven and hell, Geylang is as famed for its temples and mosques as it is for its *lorong* (alley) brothels, girly bars and cheap hotel

Changi

Heritage building, Little India

rooms. Slip in at night for brilliant street food, karaoke and a rush that's more 'cheeky Bangkok' than 'strait-laced Singapore'.

Changi & Pulau Ubin (p90)

▶ Laid-back living
▶ Changi Museum & Chapel

Laid-back Changi peddles batik fabrics, Indian textiles and harrowing stories of Singapore under Japanese occupation at the moving Changi Museum & Chapel. Further afield, bicycle-friendly Pulau Ubin island channels a long-forgotten Singapore of ramshackle huts, jungle, old plantations and quiet country lanes.

Other great places to experience the city like a local:

Chinatown Complex (p76)

Colbar (p147)

Haji Lane (p111)

Jalan Besar (p109)

MAAD (p84)

PS Cafe (p132)

Rex Cinemas (p107)

Gillman Barracks (p144)

Singapore Turf Club (p132)

Sri Muneeswaran Hindu Temple (p134)

Singapore
Day Planner

Day One

☼ Start your Singapore fling with a local breakfast of *kaya* (coconut jam) toast, runny eggs and strong *kopi* (coffee) at **Ya Kun Kaya Toast** (p77) before a riverside stroll at the **Quays** (p22) for a jaw-dropping panorama of brazen skyscrapers and refined colonial buildings. Dive into the brilliant **Asian Civilisations Museum** (p26) or keep walking to the **National Museum of Singapore** (p24) or the **Peranakan Museum** (p32) for some cultural insight, then fill up on chilli crab at riverside **Jumbo Seafood** (p150).

☼ Fingers licked, head to nearby Chinatown to feast your eyes on the technicolor **Sri Mariamman Temple** (p72) and the epic **Buddha Tooth Relic Temple** (p72). Hunt for antiques at **Far East Legend** (p84) or local art at **Utterly Art** (p84). Done, head straight up **Pinnacle@Duxton** (p75) for a cheap, incredible view of the city, or treat your feet to some reflexology at **People's Park Complex** (p73).

☽ Recharged, it's time for Southeast Asian fusion fare and killer cocktails at **Ding Dong** (p73). Dinner done, catch a taxi to the atmospheric **Night Safari** (p125), slipping into the dark for a late-night rendezvous with a cast of curious creatures.

Day Two

☼ Little India will erase every preconceived notion of Singapore as a sterile metropolis. Weathered tailors stitch and sew by the side of the road, and the air is thick with cumin and Bollywood soundtracks. Take in the colours and chanting of **Sri Veeramakaliamman Temple** (p98) and lick your fingers over lunch at **Lagnaa Barefoot Dining** (p101).

☼ Escape the afternoon heat in the air-conditioned comfort of **Orchard Rd** (p48). Hunt down rare Singaporean prints and books at **Antiques of the Orient** (p60) and cognoscenti threads at **Robinsons** (p61), **Reckless Shop** (p60), and **i.t** (p61). Shopped out, it's time for happy hour martinis at **Bar on 5** (p58) or beers on heritage beauty **Emerald Hill Rd** (p52).

☽ If you're dining at **Satay by the Bay** (p152), you're already at **Gardens by the Bay** (p28). Give yourself plenty of time to explore Singapore's incredible new botanic gardens, including the Flower Dome and Cloud Forest conservatories. The gardens' Supertrees are especially spectacular during the nightly light shows (7.45pm and 8.45pm).

Short on time?
We've arranged Singapore's must-sees into these day-by-day itineraries to make sure you see the very best of the city in the time you have available.

Day Three

☀ The golden-domed **Sultan Mosque** (p99) in Kampong Glam is the centrepiece of Singapore's historic Malay district. Explore the area's fascinating backstory at the revamped **Malay Heritage Centre** (p100), housed in a former sultan's palace, then nibble on beautiful, bubbling wood-fired pizza at nearby **Cicheti** (p103).

☀ Spend the afternoon indulging in pure, unadulterated fun on Singapore's pleasure island, Sentosa. Hit the squeal-inducing rides of **Universal Studios** (p114), or eye-up creatures great and small at the spectacular **S.E.A. Aquarium** (p117). Alternatively, ride some artificial waves at **Wave House** (p118) or book an indoor skydive at **iFly** (p118).

☾ Slow down the pace with evening drinks on a palm-fringed Sentosa beach. Options include **Coastes** (p121) or the more secluded **Tanjong Beach Club** (p121). Come dinner, go Greek at marina-side **Mykonos on the Bay** (p120). If you're travelling with kids, consider catching the popular **Songs of the Sea** (p121), a multimillion-dollar sound, light and laser show.

Day Four

☀ For a taste of 1950s Singapore, head to Changi to catch a bumboat across to **Pulau Ubin** (p90). Rent a bicycle and cycle the island's peaceful, jungle-fringed roads, passing tin-shacked houses, quirky shrines and walking along a mangrove boardwalk. There's even a mountain-bike park with trails for varying skill levels.

☀ Once you've finished exploring sleepy Pulau Ubin, catch a bumboat back to Singapore. If it's not too late, pay a visit to the moving **Changi Museum & Chapel** (p91), which recounts the suffering and resilience of those who endured Singapore's Japanese occupation. If it's too late, wander the shops at Changi Village, stopping for a beer at **Coastal Settlement** (p91).

☾ Assuming you've made a reservation, it's time for a decadent degustation dinner at French-inspired **Jaan** (p37), perched 70 floors above the city. Request a table facing Marina Bay Sands for commanding views of the spectacular nightly light and laser show. End the night at gorgeous rooftop bar **Lantern** (p40).

Need to Know

**For more information,
see Survival Guide (p174)**

Currency
Singapore dollar ($)

Languages
English, Mandarin, Malay and Tamil

Visas
Citizens of the USA, UK, Australia, New
Zealand, South Africa, most European
countries and Asean nations (except
Myanmar) do not require visas for stays
of either 30 or 90 days, depending on
the individual country. Other visitors may
require visas. See www.ica.gov.sg for
specifics.

Money
ATMs are widely available and credit
cards are accepted in all hotels and most
restaurants.

Mobile Phones
Singapore's two cell networks (GSM900
and GSM1800) are compatible with most
of the world. Buy a local SIM card to keep
costs down.

Time
Singapore Standard Time (GMT/UTC plus
eight hours)

Plugs & Adaptors
Square, three-pin plugs of the type used in the
UK; current is 220V to 240V.

Tipping
Largely unexpected and unnecessary.

① Before You Go

Your Daily Budget

Budget less than $100
► Dorm bed $20–$40
► Meal at hawker centre $3–$10
► Beer at street stall $6

Midrange $100–$350
► Double room in average hotel $100–$250
► Two-course dinner with wine $60
► Cocktail at hip bar $15–$30

Top end more than $350
► Four- and five-star double room
$250–$500
► Degustation menu at top-tier restaurant
$250-plus
► Theatre ticket $150

Useful Websites

Lonely Planet (www.lonelyplanet.com/singa-
pore) Destination low-down, hotel bookings.

Your Singapore (www.yoursingapore.com)
Tourist site with handy planning feature.

City Nomads (www.citynomads.com) Online
guide to what's hot and new in Singapore.

Advance Planning

Two months before Book tickets to the
Formula One or to short-run, Broadway-style
musicals.

One month before Book a bunk if you plan
on staying at a dorm over the weekend.
Reserve a table at a top-tier restaurant.

One week before Scan the web for last-
minute deals and upcoming festivals. Book
a cabana at rooftop bar Lantern.

② Arriving in Singapore

Changi Airport (www.changiairport.com) is one of Asia's main air hubs and Singapore's major gateway. Easy connections to central Singapore via MRT train, public and shuttle bus 5.30am to midnight, $1.85 to $9. taxi ride costs around $18 to $38. Although more expensive, a taxi from Changi Airport is by far the quicker option, no matter which part of Singapore you're staying in.A The most expensive times is between 5pm and 6am, when a whole raft of surcharges kick in. Four-seater limousine taxis cost $55 to anywhere on the island, plus $15 surcharge per additional stop. Seven-seater limousine taxis cost $60, plus $15 surcharge per additional stop. Enquire at the Ground Transport Desk at the airport.

✈ From Changi Airport

Destination	Best transport
Colonial District, the Quays & Marina Bay	MRT
Orchard Rd	bus 36
Chinatown, CBD & Tanjong Pagar	MRT
Little India & Kampong Glam	MRT
Sentosa	MRT, then Sentosa Express monorail
Holland Village & Tanglin Village	Holland Village: MRTTanglin Village: MRT, then bus 106
Southwest Singapore	MRT

③ Getting Around

Public transport is efficient, safe and relatively cheap. Buy an EZ-Link card at MRT train station counters ($12, including a $5 nonrefundable deposit) to save time and money. Cards are valid on both trains and buses, as well as in many taxis. Top up EZ-Link cards with cash or ATM cards at station ticket machines. The minimum top-up value is $10.

 MRT

Local metro with five colour-coded lines. Easiest way to get around (5.30am to midnight)

 Bus

Covers MRT areas and beyond (5.30am to midnight, plus a handful of night services).

🚗 Taxi

Safe, honest and relatively cheap. Flag one at taxi stands or try your luck on the street. Book ahead if travelling in peak hours. Hefty surcharges apply during peak hours and from midnight to 6am.

Singapore
Neighbourhoods

*Singapore Zoo &
Night Safari (12km)* ↑

Holland Village & Dempsey Hill (p126)
Latte-sipping expats, boutique antiques in converted colonial barracks and the luxurious sprawl of Singapore Botanic Gardens. You've made it, lah!

⊙ **Top Sights**
Singapore Botanic Gardens

Southwest Singapore (p138)
An urban getaway of jungle canopy walks, hilltop cocktails, historic war sites and an off-the-radar cultural gem.

⊙ **Top Sights**
Southern Ridges

Sentosa (p112)
Welcome to Fantasy Island, a 'think big' playground of theme parks, activities and shows, sunset beach bars and marina-side dining.

⊙ **Top Sights**
Universal Studios

Singapore Botanic Gardens ⊙

Southern Ridges ⊙

⊙
Universal Studios

Orchard Rd (p48)

Malls, malls, malls – from the futuristic to the downright retro, this air-conditioned thoroughfare of consumption is to retail what Las Vegas' Strip is to gambling.

Little India & Kampong Glam (p92)

The Singapore you didn't think existed: gritty, technicolor laneways bursting with spice stalls and shrines, whimsically domed mosques, sheesha cafes and independent fashion boutiques.

National Museum of Singapore

Asian Civilisations Museum

Gardens by the Bay

Chinatown Heritage Centre

Colonial District, the Quays & Marina Bay (p22)

Dashing colonial buildings, modern marvels, world-class museums and riverfront wining and dining.

⊙ **Top Sights**

National Museum of Singapore

Asian Civilisations Museum

Gardens by the Bay

Chinatown, CBD & Tanjong Pagar (p64)

A contrasting mix of incense-heady temples and sizzling hawker centres, brazen skyscrapers and revamped shophouses jammed with trendy restaurants and bars.

⊙ **Top Sights**

Chinatown Heritage Centre

Worth a Trip

⊙ **Top Sights**

Singapore Zoo

Night Safari

Explore
Singapore

Worth a Trip

Night market, Chinatown
ANDREW WATSON/GETTY IMAGES ©

Explore

Colonial District, the Quays & Marina Bay

The Colonial District dazzles with its 19th-century buildings, A-list museums and sprawling malls. Just south, the sinuous Singapore River is where you'll find the Quays and their booty of restaurants, bars and clubs. East of here, the river spills into Marina Bay, home to botanical blockbuster Gardens by the Bay and resort, casino, and entertainment-and-dining complex Marina Bay Sands.

The Sights in a Day

☀️ Start the morning with a saunter along the Singapore River, taking in Singapore's dramatic skyline. Right beside the river is the **Asian Civilisations Museum** (p26), home to a breathtaking collection of artefacts from across Asia. Done, recharge with lip-smacking chilli crab at riverside **Jumbo Seafood** (p37).

☀️ Take a postprandial stroll though refreshing **Fort Canning Park** (p33), then continue your cultural enlightenment at the **National Museum of Singapore** (p24), **Peranakan Museum** (p32) or **National Gallery Singapore** (p32), all within walking distance of the park. Alternatively, ditch the museums for a little retail therapy at malls like **Shoppes at Marina Bay Sands** (p46) and electronics nirvana **Funan DigitaLife Mall** (p46).

🌙 Nosh hawker-style at **Satay by the Bay** (p38), located at the spectacular **Gardens by the Bay** (p28). Highlights here include the Flower Dome, Cloud Forest and bird's-eye OCBC Skyway. Stay for the sound and light show, Garden Rhapsody, then cap off the evening with a rooftop toast at **Lantern** (p40) or **Orgo** (p41).

👁 Top Sights
National Museum of Singapore (p24)

Asian Civilisations Museum (p26)

Gardens by the Bay (p28)

💜 Best of Singapore
Food
Kilo (p36)

Jaan (p37)

Gluttons Bay (p37)

Jumbo Seafood (p37)

Drinking
Lantern (p40)

Bitters & Love (p40)

28 HongKong Street (p41)

Level 33 (p41)

Getting There
Ⓜ MRT City Hall (Red and Green Lines) and Dhoby Ghaut (Purple, Red and Yellow Lines) are the best MRT stops for the Colonial District. City Hall is connected via underground malls to Esplanade (Yellow Line). Raffles Place (Red and Green Lines) and Clarke Quay (Purple Line) serve the Quays. Marina Bay (Red Line) and Bayfront (Yellow and Blue Lines) service Marina Bay Sands.

Top Sights
National Museum of Singapore

Imaginative, prodigiously stocked and brilliantly designed, Singapore's National Museum is good enough to warrant two visits. At once cutting-edge and classical, the museum ditches staid exhibits for lively multimedia galleries that bring Singapore's jam-packed biography to vivid life. It's a colourful, intimate journey, spanning ancient Malay royalty and colonial-era backstabbing to 20th-century rioting, reinvention, food, fashion and film.

◉ Map p30, C1

www.nationalmuseum.sg

93 Stamford Rd

adult/child $10/5, Living Galleries free 6-8pm

⊙History Gallery 10am-6pm, Living Galleries 10am-8pm

Ⓜ Dhoby Ghaut

Don't Miss

History Gallery

Commencing with a dramatic, 360-degree video installation, the History Gallery offers an evocative multimedia journey through six centuries of Singaporean history. It's a trip that will have you peering into opium dens, eavesdropping on lunching colonial ladies and confronting harrowing tales of Japanese occupation.

Living Galleries

The 'living galleries' offer insight into modern Singaporean culture. Get the low-down on *wayang* (Javanese puppet theatre), hawker food culture, the link between fashion and women's rights, Singapore's celluloid history and intimate tales of family life.

Goh Seng Choo Gallery

Before his tenure as Singapore's first Resident and Commandant, Colonel William Farquhar (1774–1839) commissioned local artists to illustrate the flora and fauna he had discovered on the Malay Peninsula. These sumptuous watercolours now reside in the Goh Seng Choo Gallery, located beside the Living Galleries.

Art Installations & Architecture

Seven quirky art installations pimp the museum's interior and exterior. Our favourite is Kuhari Nahappan's *Pedas Pedas*, a giant bronze chilli on the lawn at the back of the complex. The chilli can be seen as a metaphor for Singapore: small and hot, yet powerful and energetic. The museum's superb neoclassical wing, built in 1887 as the Raffles Library and Museum, boasts a breathtaking rotunda, lavished with 50 panels of stained glass.

☑ Top Tips

▶ Entry is free to the Living Galleries from 6pm to 8pm daily.

▶ A 3-Day Museum Pass (adult/family $20/50) offers unlimited admission to six city museums, including this one. Passes can be purchased at the museum.

▶ The museum is a top choice for thoughtful souvenirs, with gift shop choices including Singapore tomes and locally designed objects such as tees, tote bags, and iPhone covers.

✕ Take a Break

For fusion fare, coffee or a cheeky slice of cake, head to the museum's **Food for Thought** (☻10am-9pm Mon-Sat, to 8pm Sun; Ⓜ Bras Basah, Dhoby Ghaut).

For inspired Chinese dishes, book a table at the antiques-laden **Chef Chan's Restaurant** (www.chefchanrestaurant.com.sg; ☻11.45am-2.30pm & 6.15-10.30pm; Ⓜ Dhoby Ghaut).

Top Sights
Asian Civilisations Museum

The remarkable Asian Civilisations Museum houses Southeast Asia's most comprehensive collection of pan-Asian treasures. Set over three levels, its beautifully curated galleries explore the history, cultures and religions of Southeast Asia, China, the Indian subcontinent and Islamic West Asia. Prepare to lose yourself in millennia of ancient carvings, magical swords and glittering jewels and textiles. Add to this a revealing exploration of the Singapore River and top-notch temporary exhibitions, and you have yourself one seriously satisfying cultural date.

Map p30, D4

6332 7798

www.acm.org.sg

1 Empress Pl

adult/child $8/4

10am-7pm Sat-Thu, to 9pm Fri

M Raffles Place

Don't Miss

Southeast Asia Galleries
Spanning everything from Hindu Buddhist kingdoms to hillside tribes and Javanese performing arts, highlights here include a beautifully illustrated *parabaik* (folded book), its whimsically colourful scenes a rare porthole into 19th-century Burmese life and architecture.

West Asia Galleries
Don't miss the Chinese Qur'an, which fuses both Chinese and Islamic aesthetics. Look out for the fragments from a 12th- or 13th-century Quran from southern Spain or North Africa, written in cursive Maghribi script.

China Galleries
Look for the richly hued *Three Votive Paintings of Luohan*, 18th-century silk panels portraying three sages who have realised the Buddhist doctrine (or dharmas). Equally colourful but more action-packed are the *Eight Immortals*, a 17th-century silk *kesi* (Chinese tapestry) laden with auspicious symbols.

South Asia Galleries
Beautiful artefacts include an extraordinary 17th-century gameboard made of teak and veneered with exotic woods, ivory and metals. More macabre is a 17th- or 18th-century Tibetan ritual bone apron, made using human and animal bones.

Colonial Architecture
Indian convict labour constructed the museum's home, the Empress Place Building, in 1865 for colonial government offices. It fuses neo-Palladian classicism and tropical touches: timber louvred shutters and a wide shaded porch. The original building covers Southeast Asia and South Asia.

☑ Top Tips
▶ Free, volunteer-run guided tours of selected museum highlights depart from the lobby at 11am, noon and 2pm on weekdays, and at 11am, 2pm and 3pm on weekends. There are additional tours at 1pm Monday and Thursday, and at 7pm on Friday.

▶ The National Heritage Board's 3-Day Museum Pass (adult/family $20/50) offers unlimited admission to six city museums, including this one. Passes can be purchased here.

▶ Tickets are half price from 7pm to 9pm on Friday

✕ Take a Break
The museum building is home to IndoChine Waterfront (p39), which serves fresh, zesty Southeast Asian fare, including plenty of vegetarian options.

For a drink with a view, it's an easy walk across the river to gorgeous rooftop bar Lantern (p40).

Top Sights
Gardens by the Bay

Welcome to the botanic gardens of the future, a fantasyland of space-age bio-domes, high-tech Supertrees and whimsical sculptures. Costing $1 billion and sprawling across 101 hectares of reclaimed land, Gardens by the Bay is more than just a mind-clearing patch of green. It's an ambitious masterpiece of urban planning, as thrilling to architecture buffs as it is to nature lovers.

◉ Map p30, H5

www.gardensbythebay.com.sg

18 Marina Gardens Dr

gardens free, conservatories adult/child $28/15

⊘ 5am-2am, conservatories & Skyway 9am-9pm

Ⓜ Bayfront

Don't Miss

The Conservatories

Housing 217,000 plants from 800 species, the Gardens two asymmetrical conservatories rise like giant paper nautilus shells. The larger Flower Dome replicates the dry Mediterranean climates found across the world, while the steamy Cloud Forest dome recreates the tropical montane climate found at elevations between 1500m and 3000m. Its centrepiece is a 35m mountain with waterfall.

Supertree Grove

Science fiction meets botany at the Supertrees, 18 steel-clad concrete structures adorned with over 162,900 plants. These soaring structures are actually massive exhausts for the Gardens' biomass steam turbines, used to generate electricity to cool the conservatories. For a sweeping view, walk across the 22m-high OCBC Skyway, which connects six of the Supertrees at Supertree Grove. Skyway tickets must be purchased at Supertree Grove (adult/child $5/3, cash only).

Planet Sculpture

The most visually arresting of the Gardens' numerous artworks is Mark Quinn's colossal *Planet*. Created in 2008 and subsequently donated to Gardens by the Bay, the sculpture is of a giant white seven-month-old infant, fast asleep and seemingly floating above the ground. This visual illusion is nothing short of brilliant, especially considering that the bronze bubba actually comes in at a hefty seven tonnes. The work was modelled on Quinn's very own son.

☑ **Top Tips**

▶ The best time to visit is late afternoon or early evening, when the heat softens and the Supertrees become the protagonists of the mesmerising sound and light show Garden Rhapsody, nightly at 7.45pm and 8.45pm.

▶ A **shuttle bus** (two rides $2; ⏱ 9.30am-5pm) runs every five to 10 minutes between Dragon Fly Bridge (near the entrance to Bayfront MRT station), World of Palms (alight here for Supertree Grove), the conservatories, and the Gardens' main arrival plaza and taxi stand (Carpark B). Purchase tickets on board. Services begin at 12.30pm on the first Monday of the month.

✕ **Take a Break**

Fine dine in the Flower Dome at Pollen (p39). The restaurant also hosts an excellent afternoon tea.

For a cheaper feed, opt for alfresco hawker centre Satay by the Bay (p38).

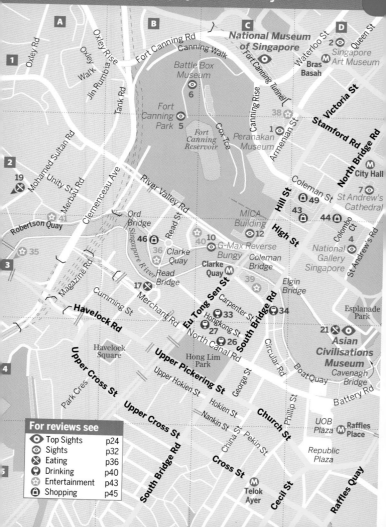

E
MINT Museum of Toys
Middle Rd
Purvis St
Bashin St
11 ⊙
24 ✕
F
Beach Rd
Seah St
Raffles Hotel
42 🔒
3 ⊙
32 🔒
Nicoll Hwy
Rochor Rd
G
14 ✕
Bras Basah Rd
Willow stream
5 ⊙ 13
30 🔒
Temasek Blvd
Temasek Ave
Promenade Ⓜ
Marina Promenade
Republic Blvd
H

1

Esplanade Ⓜ
47 🔒
Civil War Memorial Park
48 🔒
City Link Mall
Raffles Link

2

The Padang
Raffles Blvd

Connaught Dr
37 ☆
29 🔒
Raffles Ave
16 ✕
Esplanade Dr
Singapore Flyer
9 ⊙

3

Esplanade Bridge
Esplanade Jetty
Helix Bridge
East Coast Parkway

Anderson Bridge
Merlion Park

4

Collyer Quay
Fullerton Rd
25 ⊙
Marina Bay
8 ⊙
ArtScience Museum
45 🔒
23 ✕
18 ✕
20 ✕

31 ⊙

22 ✕
Bayfront Ave
MARINA SOUTH
Gardens by the Bay
⊙

5

Bayfront Ⓜ

Marina Blvd
N 0 _____ 500 m
   0 _____ 0.25 miles

Sights

Peranakan Museum
MUSEUM

1 ◎ Map p30, C2

Explore the rich, fusion heritage of the Peranakans (Straits-born locals) at this superlative museum. Thematic galleries cover various aspects of Peranakan culture, from the traditional 12-day wedding ceremony to Peranakan crafts, spirituality and feasting. Look out for extraordinarily detailed ceremonial costumes and beadwork, beautifully carved wedding beds and rare dining porcelain. An especially curious example of the Peranakans' fusion culture is a pair of Victorian bell jars, in which statues of Christ and the Madonna are adorned with Chinese-style flowers and vines. (☎ 6332 7591; www.peranakanmuseum.sg; 39 Armenian St; adult/child $6/3, half-price 7-9pm Fri, incl Asian Civilisations Museum $11/5.50; ◎ 10am-7pm, to 9pm Fri; Ⓜ City Hall)

Singapore Art Museum
MUSEUM

2 ◎ Map p30, D1

SAM houses an engaging collection of Southeast Asian art, with a strong emphasis on modern and contemporary art from Singapore and the broader Asian region. Expect anything, from painting and sculpture to site-specific installations and video art. One highlight is the Wu Guangzhong gallery, which features a rotating exhibition of $70 million worth of art donated by the father of modern Chinese painting. (SAM; ☎ 6332 3222; www.singaporeart-museum.sg; 71 Bras Basah Rd; adult/student & senior $10/5, free 6-9pm Fri; ◎ 10am-7pm Sat-Thu, to 9pm Fri; Ⓜ Bras Basah)

Raffles Hotel
HISTORIC BUILDING

3 ◎ Map p30, E1

Yes, it's a cliché, but try resisting the allure of that magnificent ivory front-age, the famous Sikh doorman and the echoes of days when Singapore was a swampy, tiger-tempered outpost of the British Empire. Starting life in 1887 as a modest 10-room bungalow fronting the beach (long gone thanks to land reclamation), Raffles is today one of Singapore's most beautiful heritage sites, laced with quiet tropical gardens, nostalgia-inducing bars and a string of high-quality art galleries and boutiques. (www.raffleshotel.com; 1 Beach Rd; Ⓜ City Hall)

National Gallery Singapore
ART GALLERY

4 ◎ Map p30, D3

When it opens in late 2015, the National Gallery Singapore will become the latest major player on the cultural circuit, not to mention the country's largest visual arts venue at 64,000 sq m. Occupying both the former City Hall and Old Supreme Court building, the complex plans to showcase the work of Singaporean and Southeast Asian artists from the 19th century to today, as well as hosting international exhibitions. See the website for updates on the gallery's opening and upcoming exhibitions.

TOMATOSKIN/GETTY IMAGES ©

ArtScience Museum (p35)

(www.nationalgallery.sg; St Andrew's Rd; Ⓜ City Hall)

Fort Canning Park   PARK

5 ◉ Map p30, B2

When Raffles rolled into Singapore and claimed it for the mother country, locals steered clear of Fort Canning Hill, then called Bukit Larangan (Forbidden Hill) out of respect for the sacred shrine of Sultan Iskandar Shah, ancient Singapura's last ruler. These days, the hill is better known as Fort Canning Park, a wonderfully lush, cool retreat from the hot streets below. Stop at the spice garden and take in the scents of tamarind and cinnamon, or ponder Singapore's wartime defeat

at the Battle Box Museum. (www.nparks. gov.sg; admission free; Ⓜ Dhoby Ghaut)

Battle Box Museum   HISTORIC SITE

6 ◉ Map p30, B1

Visit the former command post of the British during WWII and get lost in the eerie and deathly quiet 26-room underground complex. War veterans and Britain's Imperial War Museum helped recreate the authentic bunker environs; life-sized models re-enact the fateful surrender to the Japanese on 15 February 1942. Japanese Morse codes are still etched on the walls. (www.thebattlebox.com; 2 Cox Terrace; adult/child $8/5; ⊙ 10am-6pm, last entry 5pm; Ⓜ Dhoby Ghaut)

Understand
Architecture

Despite the wrecking-ball rampage of the 1960s and '70s, Singapore lays claim to a handful of heritage gems. An ever-expanding list of ambitious contemporary projects has the world watching.

Colonial Legacy

As the administrative HQ of British Malaya, Singapore gained a wave of buildings on a scale unprecedented in the colony. European aesthetics dominated, from the neoclassicism of City Hall, the Fullerton Building and the National Museum of Singapore to the Palladian-inspired Empress Building, now home to the Asian Civilisations Museum. While many other buildings adopted these styles, they were often tweaked to better suit the tropical climate, from the *porte cochère* (carriage porch) of St Andrew's Cathedral to the porticoes of the former St Joseph's Institution, current location of the Singapore Art Museum.

Shophouses

Singapore's narrow-fronted shophouses are among its most distinctive and charming architectural trademarks. Traditionally a ground-floor business topped by one or two residential floors, these contiguous blocks roughly span six styles from the 1840s to the 1960s. The true scene stealers are those built in the so-called Late Shophouse Style, with richly detailed facades often including colourful wall tiles, stucco flourishes, pilasters and elaborately shuttered windows. Fine examples grace Koon Seng Rd in Katong.

Singapore Now

Chinese American IM Pei is behind the iconic brutalist skyscraper OCBC Centre, the silvery Raffles City, and the razor-sharp Gateway twin towers. Britain's Sir Norman Foster designed the UFO-like Expo MRT station and Supreme Court, as well as the new South Beach mixed-used development (opposite Raffles Hotel), its two curving towers sliced with densely planted sky gardens. Designed by local studio Woha, the Parkroyal on Pickering hotel features dramatic hanging gardens, while Israeli-born Moshe Safdie's Marina Bay Sands turns heads with its record-breaking, 340m-long cantilevered Skypark.

St Andrew's Cathedral   CHURCH

7 ⊙ Map p30, D2

Funded by Scottish merchants and built by Indian convicts, this wedding cake of a cathedral stands in stark contrast to the glass and steel surrounding it. Completed in 1838 but torn down and rebuilt in its present form in 1862 after lightning damage, it's one of Singapore's finest surviving examples of English Gothic architecture. Interesting details include the tropics-friendly *porte cochère* (carriage porch) entrance – designed to shelter passengers – and the splendid stained glass adorning the western wall. (www.livingstreams.org.sg; 11 St Andrew's Rd; ⊙9am-5pm Mon-Sat; MCity Hall)

ArtScience Museum   MUSEUM

8 ⊙ Map p30, G4

Looking like a giant white lotus, the lily-pond-framed ArtScience Museum is well known for hosting major international travelling exhibitions in fields as varied as art, design, media, science and technology. Past shows have included retrospectives of American designers Charles and Ray Eames and photographer Annie Leibovitz. (www.marinabaysands.com/museum.html; Marina Bay Sands; adult/child $28/16; ⊙10am-7pm; MBayfront)

Singapore Flyer   VIEWPOINT

9 ⊙ Map p30, H3

Las Vegas' High Roller may have since stolen its 'World's Biggest Observation Wheel' title, but Singapore's 165m-tall ferris wheel continues to serve up a gob-smacking panorama. On a clear day, the 30-minute ride will have you peering out over the Colonial District, CBD and Marina Bay, the high-rise housing sprawl to the east and out to the ship-clogged South China Sea. Purchase tickets online for a modest discount. (www.singaporeflyer.com.sg; 30 Raffles Ave; adult/senior/child $33/24/21; ⊙ticket booth 8am-10pm, wheel 8.30am-10.15pm; MPromenade)

G-Max Reverse Bungy   ACTIVITY

10 ⊙ Map p30, C3

Prepare to be strapped into padded chairs inside a metal cage and propelled skyward to a height of 60m at speeds of up to 200km/h before being pulled back down by gravity. Though the ride offers spectacular views to those who can keep their eyes open, it's best avoided by people prone to velocity-induced vomiting. (www.gmax.com.sg; 3E River Valley Rd; per ride $45; ⊙2pm-late; MClarke Quay)

MINT Museum of Toys   MUSEUM

11 ⊙ Map p30, E1

Nostalgia rules at this slinky ode to playtime, its four skinny floors home to over 50,000 vintage toys. You'll see everything from rare Flash Gordon comics and supersonic toy guns to original Mickey Mouse dolls and oh-so-wrong golliwogs from 1930s Japan. Stock up on whimsical toys at the lobby shop or celebrate adulthood

✔️ Top Tip
Street Sculpture

If you like your art free and alfresco, the area offers a healthy crop of public sculptures by acclaimed local and international artists. At Boat Quay, UOB Plaza is home to Salvador Dali's *Homage to Newton* and Fernando Botero's *Bird*. Further east along the Singapore River, Cavenagh Bridge is the place for Chong Fat Cheong's *First Generation*. Esplanade – Theatres on the Bay claims Han Sai Por's *Seed* sculptures, while further northwest, Millenia Walk harbours Roy Lichtenstein's *Six Brushstrokes*.

with a stiff drink at the adjacent **Mr Punch Rooftop Bar**. (www.emint.com; 26 Seah St; adult/child $15/7.50; ⏱9.30am-6.30pm; Ⓜ City Hall, Bugis)

MICA Building   ART GALLERY

12 ◉ Map p30, C3

An architectural pin-up famed for its technicolor shutters and neo-Renaissance design, the MICA Building houses a string of well-known commercial art galleries representing successful regional artists. While the most famous of these is **Gajah Gallery** (www.gajahgallery.com; ⏱11am-7pm Mon-Fri, noon-6pm Sat & Sun), be sure to also pop into **Art-2 Gallery** (www.art2.com.sg; ⏱11am-7pm Mon-Sat) and **Cape of Good Hope** (☎6733 3822; www.capeofgoodhope.com.sg; 140 Hill St ; ⏱11am-7pm Mon-Sat, noon-6pm Sun; Ⓜ Clarke Quay).

Willow Stream   SPA

13 ◉ Map p30, E2

Spoil yourself silly at this lavish spa, complete with jacuzzis, plunge pools, rooms that puff aromatic steam and staff who will slather good stuff on your face before pushing, prodding and kneading the kinks out of your jetlagged (or shopped-out) body. There's also an in-house salon, covering everything from hair and waxing to manicures and pedicures. (☎6431 5600; www.willowstream.com/singapore; 80 Bras Basah Rd, Level 6, Fairmont Hotel; massage treatments from $149; ⏱7am-10pm, treatments from 9am; Ⓜ City Hall)

Eating

Kilo   FUSION $$$

14 ✕ Map p30, H1

Its location might be slightly off the radar (the 2nd floor of an industrial riverside building), but gastro geeks know exactly how to reach this cool and swinging legend. Book ahead to swoon over modern, beautifully textured dishes like salmon sushi with crunchy chicken skin, an earthy wasabi tuna tartare or sublime Italo-Japanese black-and-white prawn ravioli with sake butter. (☎6467 3987; www.kilokitchen.com; 66 Kampong Bugis; sharing plates $15-24, mains $27-39; ⏱restaurant 6-10.30pm Mon-Sat, bar 6pm-1am Wed-Sat; Ⓜ Lavender)

Jaan
FRENCH $$$

15 Map p30, E2

Perched 70 floors above the city, chic and intimate Jaan is home to French chef Julien Royer and his show-stopping, contemporary Gallic creations. From amuse-bouches like *cèpes sabayon* and mushroom tea, to protagonists like hay-roasted Bresse pigeon, flavours are revelatory and the presentation utterly theatrical. Always book ahead, and request a window seat overlooking Marina Bay Sands for a bird's-eye view of the nightly laser and light show. (6837 3322; www.jaan. com.sg; 2 Stamford Rd, Swissôtel The Stamford; lunch/dinner set menus from $68/198; noon-2pm & 7-10pm Mon-Sat, 7-10pm Sun; ; City Hall)

Gluttons Bay
HAWKER CENTRE $

16 Map p30, F3

Selected by the *Makansutra Food Guide*, this row of alfresco hawker stalls is a great place to start your Singapore food odyssey. Get indecisive over classics like oyster omelette, satay, barbecue stingray and carrot cake (opt for the black version). Its central, bayside location makes it a huge hit, so head in early or late to avoid the biggest crowds. (www.makansutra.com; 01-15 Esplanade Mall; dishes from $4; 3pm-1am Mon-Thu, to 2am Fri & Sat, to midnight Sun; Esplanade)

Jumbo Seafood
CHINESE $$$

17 Map p30, B3

If you're lusting for chilli crab – and you should be – this is a good place to indulge. The gravy is sublimely sweet and nutty, with just the right amount of chilli. Make sure you order some yeasty fried *mantou* (buns) to soak up the sauce. This branch has the best riverside location. (6532 3435; www. jumboseafood.com.sg; 30 Merchant Rd, 01-01/02 Riverside Point; dishes from $12, chilli crab around $55 per kg; noon-2.15pm & 6-11.15pm; Clarke Quay)

Kitchen at Raffles Hotel (p32)

Satay by the Bay

HAWKER CENTRE $

18 Map p30, H4

Gardens by the Bay's own hawker centre has an enviable location, alongside Marina Bay and far from the roar of city traffic. Especially evocative at night, it's known for its satay, best devoured under open skies on the spacious wooden deck. As you'd expect, prices are a little higher than at more local hawker centres, with most dishes between $8 and $10. (www.gardensbythebay.com.sg; 18 Marina Gardens Dr, Gardens by the Bay; dishes from $4; ⊙food stalls 8am-10pm, drinks stall 24hr; Ⓜ️Marina Bay, then bus 400)

Common Man Coffee

CAFE $$

19  Map p30, A2

While this airy, industrial-cool cafe roasts and serves top-class coffee, it also serves seriously scrumptious grub. Produce is super fresh and the combinations simple yet inspired, from all-day brekkie winners like green-pea fritters with crispy pancetta and balsamic syrup to a lunchtime tortilla of grilled asparagus, spiced aubergine and goat's cheese. (www.commonmancoffeeroasters.com; 22 Martin Rd, Robertson Quay; dishes $14-34; ⊙8am-6.30pm; 🖉; 🚌64, 123, 186)

Understand
Quays of the City

- -

The stretch of riverfront that separates the Colonial District from the CBD is known as the Quays.

Boat Quay (Map p30, D4) Boat Quay was once Singapore's centre of commerce, and remained an important economic area into the 1960s. The area became a major entertainment district in the 1990s, filled with tourist-targeted restaurants, bars and shops. The streets behind the main strip are infinitely more interesting, with local restaurants and somewhat seedy bars.

Clarke Quay (Map p30, B3) How much time you spend in Clarke Quay really depends upon your personal sense of aesthetics – those who love pastels will swoon, those who don't will cringe. Packed with bars, clubs and restaurants, the place is chock-a-block at night. The best ones invariably have the longest queues.

Robertson Quay (Map p30, A3) At the furthest reach of the river, Robertson Quay was once used for goods storage. Now some of the old *godown* (river warehouses) have been sexed up into flash members-only party spots and bars, though it's more low-key and grown-up than its counterparts downriver. You'll also find several savvy restaurants clustered around here.

Pollen

EUROPEAN $$$

20 Map p30, H4

Set right inside Garden by the Bay's Flower Dome, Pollen is the Singapore spin-off of Pollen Street Social, London's Michelin-starred darling. While the fine-dining restaurant delivers gorgeous, contemporary European dishes, more fun and accessible is afternoon tea in the cafe; the scones and macaroons are worth the trip alone. Book ahead (up to a week ahead on weekends). (☑6604 9988; www.pollen. com.sg; 18 Marina Gardens Dr, Flower Dome, Gardens by the Bay; mains $58-68; ☺noon-2.30pm & 6-10pm Tue-Sun, afternoon tea 3-5pm; ✍; ⓜBayfront)

IndoChine Waterfront

SOUTHEAST ASIAN $$

21 Map p30, D4

In the same building as the Asian Civilisations Museum, the IndoChine cartel's riverside operation comes with Boat Quay views and sumptuous surrounds, from Ming Dynasty–inspired chairs to glittering chandeliers. The menu is a long, sophisticated tri-nation affair of Vietnamese-, Cambodian- and Laotian-inspired dishes, with no shortage of vegetarian options. Best of all, your food comes *sans* MSG, colourings or preservatives. (☑6339 1720; www. indochine.com.sg; 1 Empress Pl, Asian Civilisations Museum; salads $17-26, mains from $18; ☺noon-3pm & 6.30-11.30pm Mon-Thu, noon-3pm & 6.30pm-12.30am Fri, 6.30pm-12.30am Sat, 6.30-11.30pm Sun; ✍; ⓜRaffles Place)

🔍 Local Life
Cult of Yet Con

Perpetually packed, **Yet Con** (Map p30, E1; 25 Purvis St; chicken rice $5.50; ☺10am-10pm; ⓜCity Hall) has been serving up superlative Hainanese chicken rice since 1940. Don't come expecting designer decor or charming service. Just come for the chicken, which is tender, full of flavour and served by stern-looking aunties to faithful suits, old-timers and geeky 20-something food nerds. Don't be put off by the crowds – turnover is fast.

Pizzeria Mozza

ITALIAN $$

22 Map p30, F5

This dough-kneading favourite is co-owned by New York super chef Mario Batali, and it's one of the few celebrity chef eateries at Marina Bay Sands that won't have you mortgaging your house. While both the antipasti and pasta dishes should appease the pickiest nonnas, the star turn is the wood-fired pizzas, with big crispy crusts to die for. (The Shoppes at Marina Bay Sands; pizzas $20-30, salads $10-22; ☺noon-11pm; ⓜBayfront)

Rasapura Masters

FOOD COURT $

23 Map p30, G4

If you prefer your hawker grub with air-con and a flanking ice-skating rink, head down to this slick, sprawling food court in the basement of the

CHRISTIAN ASLUND/GETTY IMAGES ©

Singapore Sling, Raffles Hotel (p42)

Marina Bay Sands mall. Its stalls cover most bases, from Japanese ramen and Korean kimchi to Hong Kong roast meats and local Bak Kut Teh pork-rib soup. (www.rasapura.com.sg; 2 Bayfront Ave, Level B2, The Shoppes at Marina Bay Sands; dishes from $5; MBayfront)

Jai Thai   THAI $$

24 🍽️ Map p30, E1

On a street studded with reputable eateries, lo-fi Jai Thai peddles cheap, tasty Thai under the gaze of Siamese royalty. Grab a pavement table and channel Bangkok with fragrant green curry chicken or mouth-watering fried prawns in a sweet-and-sour tamarind sauce. Like it hot? Slurp a bowl of

fiery tom yum soup (order the shrimp version). Cash only. (www.jai-thai.com; 27 Purvis St; dishes $5-16; ⏱11.30am-3pm & 6-9.30pm; MCity Hall)

Drinking

Lantern   ROOFTOP BAR

25 🍸 Map p30, E4

It may be lacking in height and serves it's drinks in plasticware (scandalous!), but Lantern remains a magical spot for a sophisticated evening toast. Why? There's the flickering lanterns, the shimmering, glass-sided pool (for Fullerton Bay Hotel guests only), and the romantic views over Marina Bay. To avoid disappointment, consider booking a table two to three days ahead. (📞6597 5299; Fullerton Bay Hotel, 80 Collyer Quay; ⏱8am-1am Sun-Thu, 8am-2am Fri & Sat; MRaffles Place)

Bitters & Love   COCKTAIL BAR

26 🍷 Map p30, C4

When the drinks are this good, you don't need signage to draw the crowds. Lurking behind top-notch eatery Shoebox Canteen, this intimate cocktail den is home to some of the city's top barkeeps, who stir, shake and slurp local-twist libations such as the rum-based, tea-infused Kaya Toast. Peckish? Swoon over buttery Wagyu Beef Cubes or get decadent with seasonal live oysters. (www.bittersandlove.com; 36 North Canal Rd; ⏱6pm-midnight Mon-Thu, to 2am Fri & Sat; MClarke Quay)

28 HongKong Street   COCKTAIL BAR

27 🍸 Map p30, C4

Softly lit 28HKS plays hide-and-seek inside an unmarked '60s shophouse. Slip inside and into a slinky scene of cosy booths and passionate mixologists turning grog into greatness. Marked with their date of origin, cocktails are seamless and sublime, among them an award-winning Whore's Bath, pimped with Baby's Breath. House-barreled classics, hard-to-find beers and lip-smacking comfort grub seal the deal. (📞6533 2001; www.28hks.com; 28 Hongkong St; ⏰5.30pm-1am Mon-Wed, to 2am Thu, to 3am Fri & Sat; Ⓜ Clarke Quay)

Level 33   MICROBREWERY

28 🍸 Map p30, E5

In a country obsessed with unique selling points, this one takes the keg. Laying claim to being the world's highest 'urban craft-brewery', Level 33 brews its own lager, pale ale, stout, porter and wheat beer. But we can live with the hyperbole as long as the views are this good and the beer crisp and cold. (www.level33.com.sg; Level 33, Marina Bay Financial Tower 1, 8 Marina Blvd; ⏰noon-midnight Sun-Thu, noon-2am Fri & Sat; 🛜; Ⓜ Downtown)

Orgo   ROOFTOP BAR

29 🍸 Map p30, E3

It's hard not to feel like the star of a Hollywood rom-com at rooftop Orgo, its view of the skyline so commanding you'll almost feel obliged to play out a tear-jerking scene. Don't. Instead, slip into a wicker armchair, order a glass of vino (hell, order a cigar as well!) and Instagram the view to the sound of soft conversation and sultry tunes. (📞6336 9366; www.orgo.sg; 8 Raffles Ave, 4th fl, Esplanade Roof Tce; ⏰6pm-1.30am; Ⓜ Esplanade)

Understand
The Singapore Sling

Granted, it tastes like cough syrup, but there's no denying the celebrity status of Singapore's most famous mixed drink. Created by Raffles Hotel barman Ngiam Tong Boon, the Singapore sling first hit the bar in 1915. It's said that the recipe was so prized that it was locked up in a safe at the hotel for years. The secret has long been out: 30mL gin, 15mL Heering cherry liqueur, 120mL pineapple juice, 15mL lime juice, 7.5mL Cointreau, 7.5mL Dom Benedictine, 10mL Grenadine, and a dash of Angostura bitters, shaken with ice, decanted into a highball glass and garnished with a cherry. In 2010 the *Straits Times* newspaper called upon Albert Yam, the great-grand-nephew of the cocktail's creator, to judge the city's best Sling. Top of the list was hotel bar **ta.ke** (Map p30, A3; Studio M Hotel, 3 Nanson Rd; ⏰6pm-1am Mon-Sat). Bottom of the list? The Sling's most famous venue, Long Bar at Raffles Hotel.

New Asia
BAR

30 Map p30, E2

Martinis demand dizzying skyline views and few deliver like this sleek bar-club hybrid, perched 71 floors above street level. A classic go-to for the cabin crew crowd, it's worth heading in early for sundowners before shaking your booty on the dance floor. Smart casual dress. (Swissôtel The Stamford, 2 Stamford Rd; admission $25; ⏰5pm-1am Sun-Tue, to 2am Wed & Thu, to 3am Fri & Sat; MCity Hall)

Understand
Kopi Culture

Single-origin beans and syphon brews may be all the rage among local hipsters, but Singapore's old-school *kopitiams* (coffeeshops) deliver the real local deal. Before heading in, it's a good idea to learn the lingo. *Kopi* means coffee with condensed milk, *kopi-o* is black coffee with sugar, while *kopi-c* gets you coffee with evaporated milk and sugar. If you need some cooling down, opt for a *kopi-peng* (iced coffee). Replace the word *kopi* with *teh*, and you have the same variations for tea. One local tea concoction worth sipping is *teh tarik* – literally 'pulled tea', it's a sweet spiced Indian tea.

Kinki
BAR

31 Map p30, E5

While Kinki's restaurant is justifiably known for its sushi, it's the rooftop bar one floor up that takes the cake. Pimped with graffiti panels and video projections, its sweep takes in Marina Bay Sands and its twice-nightly light and laser spectacular. Music levels allow for conversation and, despite the knockout location, the vibe is rarely obnoxious. (www.kinki.com.sg; 02-02 Customs House, 70 Collyer Quay; MRaffles Place)

Raffles Hotel
BAR

32 Map p30, E1

Granted, drink prices are exorbitant, but there's something undeniably fabulous about an afternoon cocktail at Singapore's most iconic hotel. Ditch the gloomy, cliched Long Bar for the fountain-graced **Raffles Courtyard** or sip Raj-style on the verandah at the **Bar & Billiard Room**. Tip: pass on the sickly sweet Singapore Sling for something more palatable, like the Autumn Sling. (www.raffles.com; 1 Beach Rd; ⏰11am-11pm; MCity Hall)

Ronin
CAFE

33 Map p30, C3

Ronin hides its talents behind a dark, tinted glass door. Walk through and the brutalist combo of grey concrete, exposed plumbing and low-slung lamps might leave you expecting some tough-talking interrogation. Thankfully,

PAUL KENNEDY/GETTY IMAGES ©

Live music, Crazy Elephant (p45)

the only thing you'll get slapped with is sucker-punch Genovese coffee, T2 speciality teas and simple, solid cafe grub like fantastic French toast and gourmet panini. Cash only. (17 Hongkong St; ◷8am-8pm Tue-Sun; Ⓜ Clarke Quay)

Actors
BAR

34 Ⓠ Map p30, C3

Every night is open-mic night at Actors, where customers are given the chance to get up and play music on one of the several assembled instruments laid out for jamming. Just the place to let your inner Elvis out! (☏6535 3270; www.actorsthejambar.com; 13A-15A South Bridge Rd; ◷6pm-2am Mon-Sat; Ⓜ Clarke Quay)

Entertainment

Zouk
CLUB

35 ⭐ Map p30, A3

Ibiza-inspired Zouk is still one of Singapore's favourite clubs, with five bars, a multilevel dance floor and no shortage of coveted, globe-trotting DJs manning the decks. You'll also find alfresco **Zouk Wine Bar**, hip-hop-centric **Phuture** and plush club-meets-lounge **Velvet Underground**, pimped with original artworks from Andy Warhol, Frank Stella and Takashi Murakami. Take a taxi and be prepared to queue. (www.zoukclub.com; 17 Jiak Kim St; ◷Zouk 10pm-late Wed, Fri & Sat, Phuture & Velvet

Shoppes at Marina Bay Sands (p46)

PETER PTSCHELINZEW/GETTY IMAGES ©

Underground 9pm-late Wed, Fri & Sat, Wine Bar 6pm-2am Tue, 6pm-3am Wed & Thu, 6pm-4am Fri & Sat; ☐5, 16, 64, 75, 123, 175, 186, 195)

Attica CLUB

36 ☆ Map p30, B3

Attica has secured a loyal following among Singapore's fickle clubbers, modelling itself on New York's hippest clubs but losing the attitude somewhere over the Pacific. Locals will tell you it's where the expats go to pick up on the weekends, mostly in the courtyard. Beats span chart hits, house, electro and R&B; check the website for themed nights. (www.attica.com.sg; 3A River Valley Rd, 01-03 Clarke Quay; ⏰Attica 10.30pm-4am Wed, Fri & Sat, to 3am Thu; Attica Too 11pm-5am Wed, 11pm-5.30am Fri & Sat; Ⓜ Clarke Quay)

Esplanade – Theatres on the Bay ARTS CENTRE

37 ☆ Map p30, E3

Home of the esteemed Singapore Symphony Orchestra (SSO), Singapore's architecturally striking arts centre includes an 1800-seater state-of-the-art concert hall, a 1940-seater theatre and an action-packed program spanning music, theatre and dance, including performances by the Singapore Dance Theatre. Check the website for upcoming events, which include regular free concerts, and don't miss an evening tipple at sultry rooftop bar Orgo (p41).

(☎ 6828 8377; www.esplanade.com; 1 Esplanade Dr; ⏰ 10am-6pm; Ⓜ Esplanade, City Hall)

Timbrè @ The Substation
LIVE MUSIC

`38` ⭐ Map p30, C1

Young ones are content to queue for seats at this popular live-music venue, whose daily rotating roster features local bands and singer-songwriters playing anything from pop and rock to folk. Hungry punters can fill up on soups, salads, tapas and passable fried standbys like buffalo wings and truffle fries. (www.timbre.com.sg; 45 Armenian St; ⏰ 6pm-1am Sun-Thu, to 2.30am Fri & Sat; Ⓜ City Hall)

Home Club
COMEDY, CLUB

`39` ⭐ Map p30, C3

While Home Club is hardly the top club in town, its Tuesday night **Comedy Masala** (comedymasala.com; adult/student $10/6 incl one drink) is a verified blast. Running from 9pm to 11.30pm, the open-mic event showcases some of the funniest, sharpest stand-up acts in town. (http://homeclub.com.sg; B1-1/06 The Riverwalk, 20 Upper Circular Rd; ⏰ 6pm-2am Tue-Thu, to 3am Fri, to 4am Sun; Ⓜ Clarke Quay)

Crazy Elephant
LIVE MUSIC

`40` ⭐ Map p30, C3

Anywhere that bills itself as 'crazy' should set the alarm bells ringing, but you won't hear them once you're inside. This touristy rock bar is beery, blokey, loud, graffiti-covered and testosterone heavy – rock on! (www.crazyelephant.com; 01-03/04, Clarke Quay; ⏰ 5pm-2am Sun-Thu, to 3am Fri & Sat; Ⓜ Clarke Quay)

Singapore Repertory Theatre
THEATRE

`41` ⭐ Map p30, A3

Based at the DBS Arts Centre, but also performing at other venues, the SRT produces international repertory standards, as well as modern Singaporean plays. The company's Shakespeare in the Park series, enchantingly set in Fort Canning Park, is deservedly popular. Check the website for upcoming productions. (☎ 6733 8166; www.srt.com.sg; DBS Arts Centre, 20 Merbau Rd; 🚌 64, 123, 143, Ⓜ Clarke Quay)

Shopping

Raffles Hotel Arcade
MALL

`42` 🔒 Map p30, E1

Part of the hotel complex, Raffles Hotel Arcade is home to some rather notable retailers. You'll find quality, affordable souvenirs at **Raffles Hotel Gift Shop** (the vintage hotel posters are great buys), high-end Singaporean and Malaysian art at **Chan Hampe** and inspired, independent fashion labels and accessories for men and women at **Front Row**. (www.raffles.com; 328 North Bridge Rd; Ⓜ City Hall)

Funan DigitaLife Mall ELECTRONICS

43 🔒 Map p30, D2

Hardwire yourself across six floors of electronics, camera and computer stores. Funan is a better bet than Sim Lim Square if you don't know exactly what you're doing. You can find almost anything at the massive **Challenger Superstore**, occupying the 6th floor. For cameras, visit family-run **John 3:16**. (www.funan.com.sg; 109 North Bridge Rd; Ⓜ City Hall)

Roxy Disc House MUSIC

44 🔒 Map p30, D2

Squeeze into Roxy's skinny aisles and scan the shelves of top-notch vinyl, both new and used, as well as CDs. Jazz and blues make up the bulk of the offerings, with both English- and Chinese-language collectors' editions thrown into the mix. You'll find the shop on the 3rd floor of The Adelphi, a lo-fi mall packed with audio equipment shops. (🕿 6336 6192; 1 Coleman St, 03-42, The Adelphi; ⏱ 1-8pm Mon-Sat, 2-8pm Sun; Ⓜ City Hall)

Shoppes at Marina Bay Sands MALL

45 🔒 Map p30, G4

You'll find all the 'it' brands at this sprawling temple of aspiration, including runway royalty such as Prada, Miu Miu and Fendi. Many people who visit cloister themselves in the dungeon-like casino, leaving the mall relatively thin on crowds – good news if you're not a fan of the Orchard Rd pandemonium. (www.marinabaysands.com; 10 Bayfront Ave; Ⓜ Bayfront)

Understand
Singlish, lah!

While Singapore's official languages are Malay, Mandarin, Tamil and English, its unofficial lingua franca is Singlish. Essentially an English dialect mixed with Hokkien, Malay and Tamil, it's spoken in a rapid, staccato fashion, with sentences polished off by innumerable but essentially meaningless exclamatory words – *lah* is the most common, but you'll also hear *mah*, *lor*, *meh*, *leh*, *hor* and several others. Other trademarks include a long stress on the last syllable of phrases, while words ending in consonants are often syncopated and vowels are distorted. What is Perak Rd to you, may well be Pera Roh to your Chinese-speaking taxi driver. Verb tenses? Forget them. Past, present and future are indicated instead by time indicators, so in Singlish it's 'I go tomorrow' or 'I go yesterday'. For more, check out the Coxford Singlish Dictionary on the satirical website **Talking Cock** (www.talkingcock.com).

Royal Selangor
GIFTS

46 🔒 Map p30, B3

Malaysia's pewter specialists might not rank high on the hip list – think the kind of personalised tankards your uncle uses for his real ale – but don't discount their jewellery, with some items that might even suit painfully fashionable teens. (www.royalselangor.com.sg; 01-01 Clarke Quay; Ⓜ Clarke Quay)

Suntec City
MALL

47 🔒 Map p30, F2

Vast, bewildering and often frustratingly inaccessible, Suntec has no shortage of retail hits, including **Uniqlo**, **Fossil**, **Kiehl's** and **Aesop**, not to mention over 50 restaurants, cafes, food courts and a sprawling branch of supermarket Giant Hyper. The star turn is the **Fountain of Wealth**, declared the World's Largest Fountain (though not Most Attractive) in the *Guinness Book of Records*. (www.suntec-city.com.sg; 3 Temasek Blvd; Ⓜ Promenade, Esplanade)

City Link Mall
MALL

48 🔒 Map p30, E2

Designed by New York's Kohn Pederson Fox, this seemingly endless tunnel of retail and food outlets links City Hall MRT station with Suntec City and the Esplanade. It's a handy means of escaping searing sun or teeming rain, and a comfortable way of getting into the city from the Marina

Q ◯ Local Life

Little Burma

Hop off at City Hall MRT station, cross North Bridge Rd, and you might just think you've hit a vertical Yangon. In truth you're in **Peninsula Plaza mall** (Map p30, D2; 111 North Bridge Rd; Ⓜ City Hall), Singapore's unofficial 'Little Burma'. Among the moneychangers, camera shops and sprawling Bata shoe shop is a legion of Burmese businesses, from visa and travel agencies to cluttered tailors and minimarts, stalls selling sweet Burmese tea, and even betel nut stands peddling folded leaves of the mild stimulant. For a mouthwatering Burmese feed, head to basement **Inle Myanmar**.

Bay hotels. (1 Raffles Link; ⊘10am-10pm; Ⓜ City Hall)

Granny's Day Out
FASHION

49 🔒 Map p30, D2

Aptly set inside très-retro Peninsula Shopping Centre, Granny's Day Out peddles a fabulous, ever-changing booty of vintage clothes, shoes and accessories from the '50s to the '80s. Sorry guys, unless you're into cross-dressing, these goods are just for the ladies. (☎6336 9774; www.grannysdayout.com; 3 Coleman St, 03-25 Peninsula Shopping Centre; ⊘noon-8pm Mon-Fri, noon-6.30pm Sun; Ⓜ City Hall)

Explore

Orchard Road

Shopping is Singapore's national sport and Orchard Rd is its Olympic-sized training ground. What was once a dusty road lined with spice plantations and orchards is now a torrent of malls, department stores and speciality shops; enough to burn out the toughest shopaholics. But wait, there's more, including drool-inducing food courts and a heritage-listed side street rocking with bars.

The Sights in a Day

☼ Breakfast at **Kith Cafe** (p55) or **Wild Honey** (p54) before stocking up on edgy local fashion at **Reckless Shop** (p60). Head west along the south side of Orchard Rd and pop into **Ngee Ann City** (p60) for books at Kinokuniya, Wisma Atria for street-chic shopping at **i.t** (p61) and futuristic **ION Orchard Mall** (p59) for macaroons at **TWG Tea** (p58). At the end of Orchard Rd, make a quick detour for **Antiques of the Orient** (p60), then head back east along the north side of Orchard Rd.

☼ For lunch, nibble, slurp and swallow Singapore's best *xiao long bao* (soup dumplings) at **Din Tai Fung** (p53) or tuck into authentic Indonesian at **Tambuah Mas** (p54), both inside luxe mall **Paragon** (p60). If you're still on a retail high, bag more cognoscenti labels at **Robinsons** (p61). Alternatively, give your body some TLC at **Tomi Foot Reflexology** (p52) or decadent **Remède Spa** (p52).

☾ After 5pm, rehydrate with cut-price martinis at **Bar on 5** (p58), kick back at **Bar Canary** (p57) or drink among heritage buildings on Emerald Hill Rd. If you don't have a reservation at Euro-Japanese superstar **Iggy's** (p53), squeeze into sushi bolthole **Wasabi Tei** (p55) for an in-the-know feed.

♥ **Best of Singapore**

Shopping
ION Orchard Mall (p59)

313@Somerset (p59)

Antiques of the Orient (p60)

Paragon (p60)

Reckless Shop (p60)

Food
Iggy's (p53)

Takashimaya Food Village (p56)

Din Tai Fung (p53)

Food Republic (p54)

Tambuah Mas (p54)

Tim Ho Wan (p54)

Wild Honey (p54)

Getting There

Ⓜ **MRT** Orchard Rd is served by no less than three MRT stations: Orchard (Red Line), Somerset (Red Line) and Dhoby Ghaut (Red, Purple and Yellow Lines). There's really no need to use other forms of transport to get here.

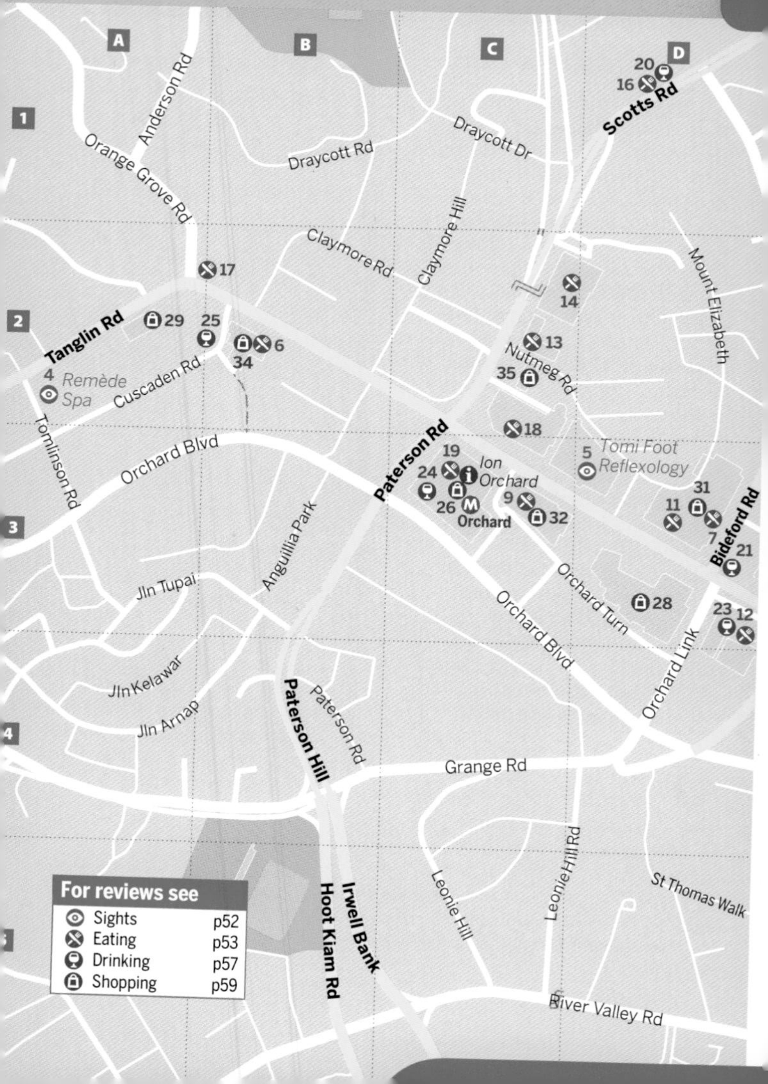
A
B
C
D
1
2
3
4
20
16
Scotts Rd
Anderson Rd
Orange Grove Rd
Draycott Rd
Draycott Dr
Claymore Hill
Claymore Rd
Mount Elizabeth
17
14
Tanglin Rd
29
25
6
34
13
Nutmeg Rd
35
4 Remède Spa
Cuscaden Rd
Tomlinson Rd
18
Paterson Rd
Orchard Blvd
19
24
Ion Orchard
26
Orchard
9
32
5 Tomi Foot Reflexology
31
11
7
Bideford Rd
21
Anguillia Park
Jln Tupai
Orchard Turn
28
23
12
Jln Kelawar
Jln Arnap
Paterson Hill
Paterson Rd
Orchard Blvd
Orchard Link
Grange Rd
Leonie Hill Rd
Leonie Hill
St Thomas Walk
Hoot Kiam Rd
Irwell Bank
River Valley Rd

For reviews see

Sights	p52
Eating	p53
Drinking	p57
Shopping	p59

E

F

G

H

Anthony Rd

Peck Hay Rd

Clemenceau Ave Nth

Monk's Hill Rd

Cairnhill Rd

Cairnhill Rise

Cavenagh Rd

Bukit Timah Rd

Istana Park

Mackenzie Rd

Cairnhill Circle

Emerald Hill Rd

Upper Wilkie Rd

Upper Wilkie Rd

Wilkie Rd

Cairnhill Rd

Saunders Rd

Hullet Rd

◎1
Emerald Hill Rd

Central Expwy

Buyong Rd

Sophia Rd

33
🔒

ℹ Orchard Road

Kramat Rd

Klok Rd

Kramat Ln

Edinburgh Rd

🔒27

Ⓜ Somerset

30 🔒

🏛22

Orchard Rd

Penang Rd

8
✕

Oldham La

Cathay Gallery

2 ◎

Handy Rd

🔒36

Exeter Rd

Eber Rd

Oxley Rd

✕10

Tan Yeok Nee House ◎ 3

Ⓜ **Dhoby Ghaut**

Devonshire Rd

Penang La

Clemenceau Ave

Fort Canning Rd

15 ✕

Killiney Rd

Oxley Rise

Canning Walk

Lloyd Rd

Fort Canning Park

500 m

0.25 miles

1

2

3

4

5

Sights

Emerald Hill Rd
NEIGHBOURHOOD

1 ◉ Map p50, F3

Take time out from your shopping to wander up frangipani-scented Emerald Hill Rd, graced with some of Singapore's finest terrace houses. Special mentions go to No 56 (built in 1902, and one of the earliest buildings here), Nos 39 to 45 (with unusually wide frontages and a grand Chinese-style entrance gate) and Nos 120 to 130 (with art deco features dating from around 1925). (Ⓜ Somerset)

Cathay Gallery
MUSEUM

2 ◉ Map p50, H4

Film and nostalgia buffs will appreciate this pocket-sized silver-screen museum, housed in Singapore's first high-rise building. The displays trace the history of the Loke family, early pioneers in film production and distribution in Singapore and founders of the Cathay Organisation. Highlights include old movie posters, cameras and programs that capture the golden age of local cinema. (www.thecathaygallery.com.sg; 2 Handy Rd, 2nd fl, The Cathay; admission free; ⏱ 11am-7pm Mon-Sat; Ⓜ Dhoby Ghaut)

Tan Yeok Nee House
NOTABLE BUILDING

3 ◉ Map p50, G4

Singapore's sole surviving example of a traditional Chinese mansion, the elegant Tan Yeok Nee House was built in 1885 as the townhouse of a prosperous merchant. Today it's part of the Asian campus of the University of Chicago Booth School of Business. While it's not open to the public, you can still admire its fine roof decoration and peek at its tranquil courtyard from the entrance. (101 Penang Rd; Ⓜ Dhoby Ghaut)

Remède Spa
SPA

4 ◉ Map p50, A2

Reputed to have the best masseurs in town, the St Regis Hotel's in-house spa is the kind of place where indulgent therapies meet chilled champagne, TWG teas and chocolates. The Wet Lounge – a marbled wonderland of a steam room, a sauna, ice fountains and jacuzzis – makes for a perfect prelude to standout treatments like the 90-minute Warm Jade Stone Massage. (☎ 6506 6896; www.remedespasingapore.com; 29 Tanglin Rd, St Regis Hotel; 1hr massages from $180; ⏱ 9am-10pm; Ⓜ Orchard)

Tomi Foot Reflexology
MASSAGE

5 ◉ Map p50, D3

Yes, that's Sting in the photo – even he knows about this no-frills massage joint, lurking in the basement of '70s throwback Lucky Plaza. Head down for one of the best rubs in town, provided by a tactile team in matching pink polos. Techniques include acupressure and shiatsu, all approved by Jesus and Mary, hanging on the wall. (304 Orchard Rd, B1-114, Lucky Plaza; 30min foot reflexology $30; ⏱ 10am-10pm; Ⓜ Orchard)

Terrace houses, Emerald Hill Rd

Eating

Iggy's INTERNATIONAL $$$

 Map p50, B2

Iggy's dark, luxe design promises something special, and head chef Akmal Anuar delivers with his arresting Italo-Japanese creations. As beautiful to look at as they are to eat, dishes here include burrata cheese paired with ginger, or soft angel hair pasta set off against crunchy sakura prawns. Mere mortals don't eat like this every day, so treat yourself. (📞6732 2234; www.iggys.com.sg; 581 Orchard Rd, Level 3, Hilton Hotel; 3-course lunch $85, set dinner menus $195-275; ⏰noon-1.30pm Mon-Fri & 7-9.30pm Mon-Sat; 🍴; MOrchard)

Din Tai Fung CHINESE $$

7 ✖ Map p50, D3

This outlet of the prolific Taiwanese chain was the first to open in Singapore. Years later, its mere mention still leaves dumpling die-hards in a drooling mess. Scan the menu and tick your choices, which should include the cult-status *xiao long bao* and the shrimp-and-pork wonton soup. The free-flow jasmine tea is a welcome touch. (www.dintaifung.com.sg; 290 Orchard Rd, B1-03/06, Paragon; buns from $1.20, dumplings from $7.30; ⏰10am-11pm; MSomerset)

Top Tip

A Green Escape

When retail fatigue creeps up on you, take solace in the rainforest. Believe it or not, you'll find one within 2km of Orchard Rd, within the grounds of the sublime Botanic Gardens. So if you're longing for a green escape from the mall madness, hop on bus 7 or 174 from the Orchard MRT exit on Orchard Blvd and you'll be breathing easy in 10 to 20 minutes.

Tim Ho Wan
CHINESE $$

8 🍴 Map p50, G4

Hong Kong's Michelin-starred dumpling peddler is now steaming in Singapore, with the same queues (head in after 8.30pm) and tick-the-boxes order form. While nothing compares to the original, the recipes are the same and the results still pretty spectacular. Must-trys include the sugary baked buns with BBQ pork and the plump prawn dumplings. (68 Orchard Rd, 01-29A/52, Plaza Singapura; dishes from $3.80; ⏲10am-10pm Mon-Fri, 9am-10pm Sat & Sun; Ⓜ Dhoby Ghaut)

Food Republic
FOOD COURT $

9 🍴 Map p50, C3

A cornucopia of local food. Muck in with the rest of the crowd for seats before joining the longest queues. Roving 'aunties' push around trolleys filled with drinks and dim sum. (435 Orchard Rd, Level 4, Wisma Atria; dishes $6-10; ⏲10am-10pm Sun-Thu, to 11pm Fri & Sat; Ⓜ Orchard)

Killiney Kopitiam
COFFEESHOP $

10 🍴 Map p50, F4

White wall tiles, fluorescent lights and endearingly lame laminated jokes: this old-school coffee joint is still *the* place for a Singaporean breakfast of *kaya* (coconut jam) toast, soft-boiled eggs and sucker-punch coffee. Post-breakfast, chow down staples like chicken curry, laksa or *nasi lemak* (coconut rice, dried anchovies and spices wrapped in a banana leaf) before sampling one of the sweet-dumpling desserts. (67 Killiney Rd; dishes $2-7; ⏲6am-11pm Mon & Wed-Sat, to 6pm Tue & Sun; Ⓜ Somerset)

Tambuah Mas
INDONESIAN $$

11 🍴 Map p50, D3

Hiding shyly in a corner of the Paragon's food-packed basement, Tambuah Mas is where Indonesian expats head for a taste of home. Bright, modern and good value, it proudly makes much of what it serves from scratch, a fact well evident in what could possibly be Singapore's best beef *rendang*. No reservations, so head in early if dining Thursday to Saturday. (☎6733 2220; www.tambuahmas.com.sg; 290 Orchard Rd, B1-44, Paragon; mains $7-25; ⏲11am-10pm; 📶; Ⓜ Somerset)

Wild Honey
CAFE $$

12 🍴 Map p50, D3

Paging Tribeca with its faux brickwork and exposed plumbing, Wild Honey peddles scrumptious, all-day breakfasts from around the world, from the tofu-laced Californian to the *shak-shouka*-spiced Tunisian. Other options include muffins and cakes, gourmet sandwiches and freshly roasted coffee. Get there before 9.30am on weekends or prepare to wait. You'll find a larger branch inside Scotts Square mall, just off Orchard Rd. (www.wildhoney.com.sg; 333A Orchard Rd, 03-02, Mandarin Gallery; breakfasts $12-24; ⊙9am-9pm, to 10pm Fri & Sat; ✐; Ⓜ Somerset)

StraitsKitchen   HAWKER CENTRE $$$

13 🍴 Map p50, C2

The hawker centre goes glam at the Grand Hyatt's highly regarded buffet, as popular with locals as it is with out-of-towners. It's a perfect introduction to classic dishes, from satay, laksa and *char kway teow* to *rendang* and *murtabak*. Come early and with an empty stomach to get value for money, and stick to the drinks included in the price (add-ons can be exorbitant). (☎6738 1234; www.singapore.grand.hyattrestaurants. com/straitskitchen; 10 Scotts Rd, Grand Hyatt; lunch/dinner buffet $45/55; ⊙noon-2.30pm & 6.30-10.30pm Mon-Fri, 12.30-3pm & 6.30-10.30pm Sat & Sun; Ⓜ Orchard)

Wasabi Tei   JAPANESE $$

14 🍴 Map p50, C2

Channelling 1972 with its Laminex countertop and wooden wall panels, this tiny, cash-only sushi bar feels like a scrumptious local secret. Stake a spot at the counter and watch the Chinese chef prove that you don't have to be Japanese to make raw fish sing

with flavour. Note: the newer sibling restaurant next door is no substitute for the original. (14 Scotts Rd, 05-70, Far East Plaza; meals $10-28; ⊙12.30-3pm & 5.30-9.30pm Mon-Fri, 12.30-4.30pm & 5.30-9.30pm Sat; Ⓜ Orchard)

Kith Cafe   CAFE $$

15 🍴 Map p50, H5

Kith kicks butt on several levels. It opens when many Singapore cafes are still snoozing, it offers free wi-fi and cool magazines, the coffee is good (they have soy!) and the grub fresh and tasty. All-day breakfast items span virtuous muesli to cheeky egg-based slap-ups, and both the salads and sandwiches pique interest with their

---

Understand
Thai'd to Tradition

With new shopping malls being shoehorned into every available space on Orchard Rd, why, many visitors ask, does the Thai embassy occupy such large, prominent grounds in an area of staggeringly expensive real estate? Back in the 1990s, the Thai government was reportedly offered $139 million for the site, but they turned it down because selling the land, bought by Thailand for $9000 in 1893 by the revered King Chulalongkorn (Rama V), would be seen as an affront to his memory. And so, happily, it remains, drooled over by frustrated developers.

gourmet combos. (✆6338 8611; kith.com.sg; 9 Penang Rd; dishes $6-24; ⏰8am-10pm Tue-Sun; 🔊🚲; Ⓜ️Dhoby Ghaut)

Buona Terra   ITALIAN $$$

16 🍴 Map p50, D1

You'll find no more than 10 linen-lined tables at this good-looking Italian. In the kitchen, young Lombard chef Denis Lucchi turns exceptional ingredients into elegant, modern dishes such as house-made pappardelle pasta with wagyu short ribs, morel and Fontina cream. Lucchi's right-hand man is Emilian sommelier Gabriele Rizzardi, whose wine list, though expensive, is extraordinary. (✆6733 0209; www.scotts29.com/buonaterra; 29 Scotts Rd; 3/4/5/6 courses $88/108/128/148; ⏰6-10.15pm Mon-Sat; Ⓜ️Newton)

Bodega y Tapas   TAPAS $$

17 🍴 Map p50, B2

At a busy junction, this contemporary bar-bistro channels España with breezy guitar riffs, splashes of Spanish red and beautiful tapas. Portions are generous (three tapas per person should suffice) and flavours simple and satisfying. The Iberico ham croquettes are velvety perfection, while the sizzling garlic prawns come with a welcome baguette to mop up all that oily, garlicky goodness. (esmirada.com; 442 Orchard Rd; tapas $7-19, mains $22-44; ⏰noon-1am Mon-Sat, to midnight Sun; Ⓜ️Orchard)

Providore   CAFE $$

Waiting for you at the top of Mandarin Gallery's outdoor escalator, in the same building as Wild Honey (see **12** 🍴 Map p50, D3), is the Providore: a cool, upbeat cafe pimped with white tiles, industrial details and shelves neatly stocked with gourmet pantry fillers. Sip a full-bodied latte or scan the menu for an all-bases list of options, from organic muesli and pancakes to gourmet salads, sandwiches and a carbalicious lobster mac and cheese. (✆6732 1565; www.theprovidore.com; 333A Orchard Rd, 02-05, Mandarin Gallery; dishes $8.50-26.50; ⏰9am-10.30pm; 🔊; Ⓜ️Somerset)

Local Life
Food Court Flavours

Burrow into the basement of most malls on Orchard Rd and you'll find a food court with stall upon stall selling cheap, freshly cooked dishes from all over the world. One of the best is slick, sprawling **Takashimaya Food Village** (Map p50, D3; 391 Orchard Rd, B2, Takashimaya Department Store, Ngee Ann City; snacks from $1; ⏰10am-11pm; Ⓜ️Orchard), which serves up a who's who of Japanese, Korean and other Asian culinary classics. Look out for *soon kueh* (steamed dumplings stuffed with bamboo shoots, bangkwang, dried mushroom, carrot and dried prawn), and don't miss a fragrant bowl of noodles from the Tsuru-koshi stand.

Mustard Incident AMERICAN $

 Map p50, C2

Lurking in the basement of Tangs department store, this hole-in-the-wall hot-dog vendor makes all its sausages, condiments and sauces from scratch. Bust your jaw on the epic Frankenstein (pork and beef sausage, streaky bacon, chilli, garlic sauce and hot sauce) or go lighter with the satisfying Chicago dog, topped with fresh diced tomato. (310 Orchard Rd, B1, Tangs Orchard; hot dogs $9-10; 10.30am-9.30pm Mon-Thu & Sat, to 11pm Fri, 11am-8.30pm Sun; M Orchard)

Gelateria Italia ICE CREAM $

 Map p50, C3

Lick yourself silly at this mouth-watering gelato stall, deep within the bowels of ION Orchard mall. Free of nasty chemicals, preservatives and artificial colours or flavours, its luscious offerings include an obscenely rich dark truffle chocolate and a pistachio that – wait for it – actually tastes like pistachio! (2 Orchard Turn, B4-K1, ION Orchard; ice cream from $5.40; 11am-10.30pm; M Orchard)

Drinking

Néktar BAR

20 Map p50, D1

Think Néktar and think well-crafted cocktails in an intimate, colonial setting. Sink into a wicker chair on the back patio with a Cointreau-spiked,

Shopping centre food court

bitter chocolate martini. Admittedly, the drinks are pricier than at many comparable venues, but the romantic setting makes for a blissful escape from Orchard Rd's overstimulation. (nektar.com.sg; 31 Scotts Rd; 5pm-1am Mon-Fri, to 2am Sat; M Newton)

Bar Canary BAR

21 Map p50, D3

Canary yellow sofas, tropical foliage and the evening sound of humming traffic and screeching birds – alfresco Bar Canary hovers high above the Orchard Rd madness. It's a chic, moody spot for an evening tipple, with attentive staff and well-positioned fans. Book six weeks ahead for their legendary Wednesday Ladies' Night deal: free-flow Veuve followed by half-priced drinks all night. (www.park-hotelgroup.com/orchard/dining/bar-canary; 270 Orchard Rd, entry on Bideford Rd, Park Hotel Orchard; ⊙noon-1am Sun-Thu, to 2am Fri & Sat; Ⓜ Somerset)

KPO   BAR

22 Ⓣ Map p50, F4

It may no longer be such a see-and-be-seen place, but KPO remains a solid spot to kick back with a beer, especially on the rooftop terrace. It's a contemporary tropical space, with concrete walls, timber detailing and no shortage of greenery. It's also the only bar in town with an attached post office. (www.imaginings.com.sg; 1 Killiney Rd; ⊙4pm-1am Mon-Thu, to 2am Fri, 6pm-2am Sat; Ⓜ Somerset)

Ⓠ Local Life
Emerald Hill Rd

Housed in century-old Peranakan shophouses, Emerald Hill Rd's cluster of bars are popular with the after-work crowd. Top billing goes to neon-pimped **Ice Cold Beer** (Map p50, E3; 9 Emerald Hill Rd; ⊙5pm-2am Sun-Thu, to 3am Fri & Sat; Ⓜ Somerset), a raucous, boozy dive bar with dart boards, a pool table and tongue-in-cheek soft-core pinups on the wall. It's a come-as-you-are kind of place where you don't have to be 20-something to have a rocking good time. Good happy-hour deals run from 5pm to 9pm, and it's especially kicking on Friday nights.

Bar on 5   BAR

23 Ⓣ Map p50, D3

This slinky hotel bar has one of the best happy hour deals in town: smooth, well-crafted martinis for under $10 a pop. Purists should forego the flavoured versions on the menu and request a classic dry instead. Drink specials run from 5pm to 9pm, accompanied by a largely middle-management crowd and eclectic tunes spanning ABBA to Rihanna. (333 Orchard Rd, Mandarin Orchard; ⊙11am-1am Sun-Thu, to 2am Fri & Sat; Ⓜ Somerset)

TWG Tea   CAFE

24 Ⓣ Map p50, C3

Posh tea purveyor TWG peddles over 800 single-estate teas and blends from around the world, from English Breakfast to Rolls Royce varieties like Da Hong Pao from Fujian. Savour the flavour with a few tea-infused macarons – the *bain de roses* is divine. There's a second outlet one floor down. (www.twgtea.com; 2 Orchard Rd, 02-21, ION Orchard; ⊙10am-10pm; Ⓜ Orchard)

Cuscaden Patio   BAR

25 Ⓣ Map p50, B2

This rundown basement bar with a small, open-air patio shouldn't be any good, but extra-friendly staff and extra-cheap drinks ensure it's as popular as any of the shiny bars around Orchard Rd. Cut-price beer deals mean you can sink a mug of San Miguel for as little as $5.90. On Tuesday nights, jugs of beer are yours

ION Orchard Mall

for $13. (21 Cuscaden Rd, B1-11, Ming Arcade; ⏰3pm-1am Mon, Wed & Thu, to 2am Tue, to 3am Fri & Sat; Ⓜ Orchard)

Shopping

ION Orchard Mall   MALL

26 🔒 Map p50, C3

Futuristic ION is the cream of Orchard Rd malls. Rising directly above Orchard MRT Station, its cleverly designed floors are busy without feeling packed. Basement floors focus on mere-mortal high-street labels like Zara and Uniqlo, while upper-floor tenants read like the index of *Vogue*. The attached 56-storey tower offers a top-floor, take-it-or-leave-it viewing gallery, **ION Sky** (www.ionsky.com.sg; ticket counter level 4; adult/child $16/8; ⏰10am-noon & 2-8pm). (www.ionorchard. com; 430 Orchard Rd; ⏰10am-10pm; Ⓜ Orchard)

313@Somerset   MALL

27 🔒 Map p50, E4

Right above Somerset MRT, young and vibrant 313@Somerset delivers affordable, popular fashion and lifestyle brands, including Uniqlo, Zara, Cotton On, Aldo and Muji. It's also home to the ever-busy Apple shop, EpiCentre, as well as cafes and restaurants. (www.313somerset.com.sg; 313 Orchard Rd; Ⓜ Somerset)

Local Life

Qisahn

Local gaming geeks swarm to **Qisahn** (Map p50, B2; www.qisahn.com; 545 Orchard Rd, 05-13, Far East Shopping Centre; ⏲noon-8pm; Ⓜ Orchard), a tiny store famed for undercutting the competition. Hidden away in Far East Shopping Centre, the place sells both new and pre-loved video games for all major platforms, including Nintendo Wii, Sony Playstation, Xbox 360 and PC. You can check available games on their website, and don't forget – they will match any competitor's price.

Ngee Ann City   MALL

28 🔒 Map p50, D3

It might look like a foreboding mausoleum, but this marble-and-granite behemoth promises retail giddiness on its seven floors of stores. International luxury brands compete for space with bookworm-nirvana **Kinokuniya** (Southeast Asia's second-largest bookstore) and the Japanese department store **Takashimaya**, home to Takashimaya Food Village, one of the strip's best food courts. (www.ngeeanncity.com.sg; 391 Orchard Rd; ⏲10am-9.30pm; Ⓜ Orchard)

Antiques of the Orient   ANTIQUES

29 🔒 Map p50, A2

Snugly set in a mall filled with Asian arts and crafts shops, Antiques of the Orient is a veritable treasure chest of original and reproduction vintage prints, photographs and maps from across the continent. Especially beautiful are the richly hued botanical drawings commissioned by British colonist William Farquhar. (www.aoto.com.sg; 19 Tanglin Rd, 02-40, Tanglin Shopping Centre; ⏲10am-6pm Mon-Sat, 11am-4pm Sun; Ⓜ Orchard)

Reckless Shop   FASHION

30 🔒 Map p50, F4

Young, talented local designer Afton Chan thrills fashion fiends with her highly creative, affordable creations. There are three labels. Entry-level Odds focuses on street-chic womenswear, while midrange Still delivers svelte, professional pieces for working women. Most impressive, however, is main label Reckless Ericka, which melds classic tailoring with fantastical, fashion-forward aesthetics inspired by themes as diverse as photography and Japanese anime. (www.recklessericka.com; 181 Orchard Rd, 02-08/09, Orchard Central; ⏲11am-9.30pm; Ⓜ Somerset)

Paragon   MALL

31 🔒 Map p50, D3

Even if you don't have a Gold Amex, strike a pose inside this Maserati of Orchard Rd malls. Status labels include Burberry, Hermès, Jimmy Choo, and Singapore's own **Raoul**, which offers sharp, detailed men's threads and crisp, invigorating womenswear, from classic cropped trousers to sassy cocktail frocks. High-street brands include Banana Republic, G-Star Raw and Miss Selfridge. (www.paragon.com.sg; 290 Orchard Rd; ⏰10am-9pm; Ⓜ Somerset)

i.t

FASHION

32 🔒 Map p50, C3

Hong Kong concept store i.t has sexed up the Singapore scene with its booty of high-end, avant-garde street wear labels for men and women. Labels include Izzue, 5cm, Judith Katie and tout à coup, with everything from denim, frocks and T-shirts to sneakers and heels. (www.itlabels.com.sg; 435 Orchard Rd, 03-15, Wisma Atria; ⏰10.30am-10pm; Ⓜ Orchard)

Robinsons

DEPARTMENT STORE

33 🔒 Map p50, E3

Robinsons' arresting, light-filled flagship should be high on any fashionista's hit list. The department store's fashion edits are sharp and inspired, pairing well-known 'it' labels like Chloe, Coach and Dior with lesser-known cognoscenti brands such as South Korea's Brownbreath, Denmark's Vito and Italy's MSGM. Clothes and kicks aside, you'll find anything from Claus Porto soaps to classic Danish design. (www.robinsons.com.sg; 260 Orchard Rd; ⏰10.30am-10pm; Ⓜ Somerset)

Forum

MALL

34 🔒 Map p50, B2

Peaceful, light-filled Forum eschews obvious brands for more discerning offerings. Deep-pocketed, fashion-forward women score playful, progressive pieces at **Tsumori Chisato**,

while fashion-literate guys and girls bag hip, make-a-statement threads and footwear at **Club 21**. One floor up is a string of boutiques dedicated to designer kids' clothing and quality toys. (www.forumtheshoppingmall.com.sg; 583 Orchard Rd; ⏰10am-10pm; Ⓜ Orchard)

On Pedder

SHOES, ACCESSORIES

35 🔒 Map p50, C2

Even if you're not in the market for high-end heels and bags, On Pedder thrills with its creative, whimsical items. The store hand picks only the most unique pieces from leading designers, whether it's ice-cream-cone stilettos from Charlotte Olympia or embroidered, book-shaped clutches from Olympia Le-Tan. Accessories include statement jewellery fit for a modern gallery. (www.onpedder.com; 6 Scotts Rd, Scotts Square; ⏰10am-10pm; Ⓜ Orchard)

Rockstar

FASHION

36 🔒 Map p50, H4

You'll find both major and independent labels at Rockstar, well known for its fun, youthful showcase of threads, shoes and accessories. Men's items range from quirky shirts to statement espradilles. The women's collection is bigger ranging from whimsical party frocks and little black dresses to statement swimwear, candy-coloured sneakers and detail-focussed jewellery. (www.rockstarsingapore.blogspot.com.au; 22 Orchard Rd; ⏰11.30am-9.30pm; Ⓜ Dhoby Ghaut). **Cathay Cineleisure** (Map p50, D4; 8 Grange Rd, 03-08; ⏰noon-10pm; Ⓜ Somerset) has another branch.

Local Life
Tiong Bahru

Getting There

Ⓜ MRT Catch the subway to Tiong Bahru, walk east along Tiong Bahru Rd for 350m, then turn right into Kim Pong Rd.

Spend a weekend morning in Tiong Bahru, Singapore's current epicentre of independent cool. An easy three stops from Raffles Place MRT station, it's more than just an ever increasing list of eclectic boutiques, bookstores, cafes and bakeries that make this low-rise neighbourhood worth a saunter. This area was Singapore's first public housing estate, its streetscape of walk-up, art deco apartments now among the city's most unexpected architectural treats.

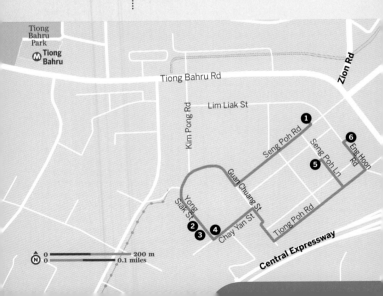

1 Market & Food Centre

The **Tiong Bahru Market & Food Centre** (83 Seng Poh Rd; ⊙8am-late, individual stalls vary) remains staunchly old-school, down to its orange-hued exterior, the neighbourhood's original shade. Its hawker centre is home to cultish **Jan Bo Shui Kueh** (02-05, Tiong Bahru Market & Food Centre; shui $1.20-3.30; ⊙6.30am-10.30pm), famous for its *chwee kueh* (steamed rice cake with diced preserved radish).

2 BooksActually

Bibliophilic bliss, **BooksActually** (www.booksactually.com; 9 Yong Siak St; ⊙11am-6pm Mon, 11am-9pm Tue-Fri, 10am-9pm Sat, 10am-6pm Sun; MTiong Bahru) is Singapore's coolest independent bookstore, with an unusual range of fiction and nonfiction, including some interesting titles on Singapore. For beautiful children's books, check out **Woods in the Books** (www.woodsinthebooks.sg; 3 Yong Siak St; ⊙11am-8pm Tue-Sat, 11am-6pm Sun), three doors down.

3 Strangelets

Strangelets (www.strangelets.sg; 7 Yong Siak St; ⊙11am-8pm Mon-Fri, 10am-8pm Sat & Sun) is an attractively curated design store filled with quirky local jewellery, French candles, Florentine soaps, Swedish socks, Californian bags and rucksacks. Try the blood orange and rosemary organic Popaganda popsicles.

4 Nana & Bird

Around the corner is **Nana & Bird** (www.nanaandbird.com; 79 Chay Yan St, 01-02; ⊙noon-7pm Tue-Fri, 11am-7pm Sat & Sun). Originally a pop-up concept store, it's now a Tiong Bahru staple, with forward fashion, accessories and art. Find unexpected brands like Singapore's Aijek and By Invite Only. The newer, nearby **flagship store** (59 Eng Hoon St, 01-65; ⊙noon-7pm Tue-Fri, 11am-7pm Sat & Sun) includes kidswear.

5 Fleas & Trees

Ubercool vintage store **Fleas & Trees** (01-10, 68 Seng Poh Lane; ⊙6-10pm Tue-Thu, 10am-10pm Fri-Sun) occupies a converted cold storage. At the helm is husband-and-wife team Terrence Yeung and Bella Koh, who scour the world for fab eclectic homewares, whimsical fashion, jewellery, books and magazines.

6 Tiong Bahru Bakery

Get some French lovin' at baker Gontran Cherrier's cool, contemporary **Tiong Bahru Bakery** (☎6220 3430; www.tiongbahrubakery.com; 56 Eng Hoon St, 01-07; pastries from $3, sandwiches & focaccias from $8; ⊙8am-10pm). Faultless pastries include buttery almond brioche, while savouries include salubrious sandwiches exploding with prime ingredients. Topping it off is beautiful coffee from Common Man Roasters.

Explore

Chinatown, CBD & Tanjong Pagar

These 'hoods keep things interesting with diverse architecture, culinary riches and top-notch bars. Not huge on must-see sights, it's about the vibe. Dive into Chinatown for wet markets, hawker food and temples, and into the CBD to sip and party in converted banks. South of Chinatown, Tanjong Pagar is great for contemporary galleries, artisan coffee, cocktails and heritage shophouses.

Sights in a Day

☀ Breakfast at veteran **Ya Kun Kaya Toast** (p77), then get the dirt on the area's past at the **Chinatown Heritage Centre** (p66). Picture those opium dens as you saunter down Pagoda St to bursting-with-colour **Sri Mariamman Temple** (p72). Across the street, scour for antiques at **Far East Legend** (p84) and Chinese remedies at **Eu Yan Sang** (p85).

☀ Hunt down a table at **Maxwell Road Hawker Centre** (p76) and taste-test the city's legendary street food, then lose yourself in the glittering excess of the **Buddha Tooth Relic Temple** (p72). Collect your thoughts on the rooftop garden, before making your way to **Yixing Xuan Teahouse** (p82) for old-school tea and nibbles. Alternatively, treat yourself to a little pampering at cut-price Mr Lim Foot Reflexology at **People's Park Complex** (p73).

☾ Come dinner, opt for contemporary Southeast Asian flavours at **Ding Dong** (p73), killer crab at **Momma Kong's** (p75) or sexy Mexican at sceney **Luca Loco** (p75). Either way, end the evening taste-testing some of Singapore's top cocktail bars, among them **Tippling Club** (p78) and **Jekyll & Hyde** (p78), or catch a rooftop breeze at **Breeze** (p80).

For a local's day in Chinatown, see p68.

◉ Top Sights

Chinatown Heritage Centre (p66)

◯ Local Life

Chinatown Tastebuds & Temples (p68)

♥ Best of Singapore

Museums

Chinatown Heritage Centre (p66)

Baba House (p72)

Food

Ding Dong (p73)

Momma Kong's (p75)

Lucha Loco (p75)

Drinking

Tippling Club (p78)

Jekyll & Hyde (p78)

Getting There

Ⓜ **MRT** Alight at Chinatown (Purple and Blue Lines) for Chinatown, Raffles Place (Red and Green Lines) or Telok Ayer (Blue Line) for CBD, and Tanjong Pagar (Green Line) or Outram Park (Purple and Green Lines) for Tanjong Pagar, including Duxton Hill.

🚌 **Bus** The 61, 145 and 166 link Chinatown to the Colonial District.

Top Sights
Chinatown Heritage Centre

Spread across three floors of three adjoining shophouses, the Chinatown Heritage Centre lifts the lid on Chinatown's chaotic, colourful and often scandalous past. While its production values can't match those of the city's blockbuster museums, its endearing jumble of old photographs, personal anecdotes and recreated environments deliver an evocative stroll through the neighbourhood's highs and lows. Spend some time in here and you can expect to see Chinatown's now tourist-conscious streets in a much more intriguing light.

👁 Map p70; D2

📞 6221 9556

www.singaporechinatown.com.sg

48 Pagoda St

adult/child $10/6

🕐 9am-8pm

Ⓜ Chinatown

Don't Miss

Roots Exhibition

Although Chinatown was allocated to all Chinese traders in the Raffles Plan of 1828, the area was further divided along ethnic lines: Hokkien on Havelock Rd and Telok Ayer, China and Chulia Sts; Teochew on Circular Rd, Boat Quay and Upper South Bridge Rd; and Cantonese on Upper Cross St and Lower South Bridge and New Bridge Rds. This section of the museum explores the experiences of these migrants, from their first impressions to the important role played by the area's clan associations.

Recreated Cubicles

The museum's faithful recreation of old Chinatown's cramped living quarters is arguably its best feature. Faithfully designed according to the memories and stories of former residents, the row of claustrophobic cubicles will have you peering into the ramshackle hang-outs of opium-addicted coolies, stoic Samsui women and even a painter and his family of 10! It's a powerful sight, vividly evoking the tough, grim lives that many of the area's residents endured right up to the mid-20th century.

Recreated Tailor Shop & Living Quarters

The time travel continues one floor down, where you'll stumble across a recreated tailor shopfront, workshop and living quarters. By the early 1950s, Pagoda St was heaving with tailor shops and this is an incredibly detailed replica of what was once a common neighbourhood. Compared to the cubicles upstairs, the tailor's living quarters appear relatively luxurious, with separate quarters for the tailor's family and apprentices, and a private kitchen.

☑ **Top Tips**

► Keep in mind that last entry into the museum is at 7pm.

► The ground-floor gift shop usually stocks cool vintage postcards and mounted old photographs of Singapore.

✗ **Take a Break**

Avoid the tourist-trap eateries on Pagoda St. Instead, join gluttonous locals at the upstairs hawker centre at Chinatown Complex (p76).

If it's after 5pm, walk over to Club St and adjoining Ann Siang Rd for a swinging happy-hour scene and top-notch, contemporary dining at Ding Dong (p73).

Local Life
Chinatown Tastebuds & Temples

Considering its past as a hotpot of opium dens, death houses and brothels, it's easy to write off today's Chinatown as a paler version of its former self. Yet beyond the tourist tack that chokes Pagoda, Temple and Trengganu Sts lies a still-engrossing neighbourhood where life goes on as it has for generations, at cacophonous market stalls, retro *kopitiams* (coffeeshops) and historic temples.

1 Chinatown Wet Market

Elbow aunties at the famous **Chinatown Wet Market** (11 New Bridge Rd, Chinatown Complex; ⏱5am-noon), in the basement of the Chinatown Complex. At its best early in the morning, it's a rumble-inducing feast of wriggling seafood, exotic fruits and vegetables, Chinese spices and preserved goods.

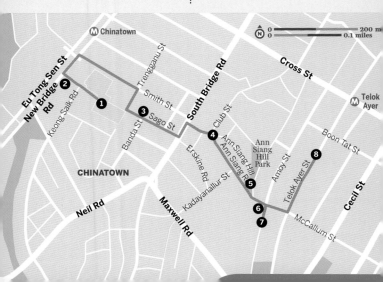

❷ Tiong Shian Porridge Centre

Appetite piqued, pull up a plastic stool at **Tiong Shian Porridge Centre** (265 New Bridge Rd; porridge $3.50-5.20; ⏱8.30am-4am), an old-school *kopitiam* where old uncles tuck into delicious congee. Winners here include porridge with century egg and pork, and the speciality claypot frog leg porridge. Each order is made fresh.

❸ Chop Tai Chong Kok

Pick up something sweet at **Chop Tai Chong Kok** (34 Sago St; pastries from $0.60; ⏱10am-6pm), a supertraditional pastry shop in business since 1938. If you're undecided, opt for the speciality lotus-paste mooncakes. Once known for its sago factories and brothels, Sago St itself now peddles everything from barbequed meat to pottery.

❹ Ann Siang Road & Club Street

A quick walk away is trendy Ann Siang Rd, well known for its restored heritage terraces and booty of fashionable restaurants, bars and boutiques. Architecture buffs will appreciate the art deco buildings at Nos 15, 17 and 21 and adjacent Club Street, also famed for its old shophouses, trendy bars, eateries and after-work buzz.

❺ Ann Siang Hill Park

At the top of Ann Siang Rd is the entrance to Ann Siang Hill Park. Not only is this Chinatown's highest point, it's a surprising oasis of green in the centre of the city. Kick back on a bench, catch the skyline through the foliage and follow the walkways downward to Amoy St.

❻ Siang Cho Keong Temple

Small Taoist **Siang Cho Keong Temple** (66 Amoy St; ⏱7.30am-5pm) was built by the Hokkien community in 1867–69. Left of the temple entrance you'll see a small 'dragon well': drop a coin and make a wish. The temple gets particularly busy at lunchtime when the faithful file in to offer incense and prayers.

❼ Rafee's Corner

Time for a quick pit stop at **Rafee's Corner** (7 Maxwell Rd, Amoy Street Food Centre, stall No 02-85; ⏱6.30am-6pm Mon-Fri, to 2pm Sat & Sun), a humble tea vendor inside Amoy Street Food Centre. If he's in a good mood, the owner might overexaggerate the pulling. This is your cue to laugh.

❽ Telok Ayer Street

In Malay, Telok Ayer means 'Water Bay', and Telok Ayer St was indeed a coastal road until land reclamation efforts in the late 19th century. Among its famous residents is Al-Abrar Mosque, built in the 1850s, Thian Hock Keng Temple, the oldest Hokkien temple in Singapore, and the Nagore Durgha Shrine, a mosque built between 1828 and 1830 by Chulia Muslims from south India.

A

B

C

D

1

Pearl's Hill
Reservoir

Pearl's Hill
City Park

Park Cres

People's
Park Complex
◉ 6

45
🔒

Upper Cross St

Chinatown
Heritage
Centre
🔒 40

Ⓜ Chinatown

◉

Pagoda St

2

Pearl's Hill Tce

Eu Tong Sen St

New Bridge Rd

Temple St

Trengganu St

Smith St

44

⊗ 12

23

Pearl Bank

Sago St

☆ 35

Banda St

3

Ⓜ Outram
Park

Keong Saik Rd

Kreta Ayer Rd

Buddha Tooth
Relic Temple

Spring St

South Bridge Rd

3
◉ 19

CHINATOWN

4

Ⓜ Outram
Park

Teck Lim Rd

Chuan Rd

34 🚌

☆ 38

⊗ 9

Duxton Hill

15

⊗ 11

Singapore
City Gallery

32

20

Murray St

Murray Tce

Maxwell Rd

Outram Rd

Bukit Pasoh Rd

Cook St

Duxton Rd

Tanjong Pagar Rd

Tras St

Peck Seah St

5

◉ 1

Everton
Park

Neil Rd

Cantonment
Rd

43 🔒

33

**TANJONG
PAGAR**

⊗ 10

21

Craig Rd

E

F

G

H

Church St

Chulia St
27

UOB
Plaza

Hokien St

Nankin St

Chin Chew St

China St

Phillip St

Market St

Malacca St

Republic
Plaza

D'Almeida St

8
Mosque St

Pekin St

16

Amoy St

Telok Ayer St

Sri Mariamman
Temple

2

39   28

25

Cross St

Telok
Ayer

Cecil St

24

42

30

41

Market St

Robinson Rd

Club St

22

13

37
29   31

18

Boon Tat St

Ann Siang Hill

Ann
Siang
Hill
Park

Thian Hock
Keng Temple
4

36

17

Erskine Rd

26

7

14

Amoy St

Telok Ayer St

Stanley St

Robinson Rd

Maxwell Link

Raffles Quay

McCallum St

MARINA
SOUTH

Maxwell Rd

For reviews see

🟠	Top Sights	p66
⊙	Sights	p72
✖	Eating	p73
🟢	Drinking	p78
✪	Entertainment	p83
🔒	Shopping	p84

N 0   200 m
   0   0.1 miles

Sights

Baba House   MUSEUM

1 ◎ Map p70, A5

Baba House is one of Singapore's best-preserved Peranakan heritage homes. Built in the 1890s, it's a wonderful window into the life of an affluent Peranakan family living in Singapore a century ago. Its loving restoration has seen every detail attended to, from the carved motifs on the blue facade down to the door screens. The only way in is via an excellent guided tour, held every Monday, Tuesday, Thursday and Saturday. Bookings, by telephone, are essential. (☑6227 5731; www.nus.edu. sg//cfa/museum; 157 Neil Rd; admission free; ☉1hr tours 2pm Mon, 6.30pm Tue, 10am Thu, 11am Sat; Ⓜ Outram Park)

Sri Mariamman Temple   HINDU TEMPLE

2 ◎ Map p70, E2

Paradoxically in the middle of China-town, this is the oldest Hindu temple in Singapore, originally built in 1823, then rebuilt in 1843. You can't miss the fabulously animated, technicolor 1930s *gopuram* (tower) above the entrance, the key to the temple's South Indian Dravidian style. Sacred cow sculptures graze the boundary walls, while the *gopuram* is covered in kitsch plasterwork images of Brahma the creator, Vishnu the preserver and Shiva the destroyer. (244 South Bridge Rd; ☉7am-noon & 6-9pm; Ⓜ Chinatown)

Buddha Tooth Relic Temple   BUDDHIST TEMPLE

3 ◎ Map p70, D3

Consecrated in 2008, this hulking, five-story Buddhist temple is home to what is reputedly the left canine tooth of the Buddha, recovered from his funeral pyre in Kushinagar, northern India. While its authenticity is debated, the relic enjoys VIP status inside a 420kg solid-gold stupa in a dazzlingly ornate 4th-floor room. The peaceful rooftop garden features a huge prayer wheel inside a 10,000 Buddha Pavilion. (www. btrts.org.sg; 288 South Bridge Rd; ☉7am-7pm, relic viewing 9am-6pm; Ⓜ Chinatown)

Thian Hock Keng Temple   TAOIST TEMPLE

4 ◎ Map p70, F3

Oddly, while Chinatown's most famous Hindu temple is swamped, its oldest and most important Hokkien temple is often a haven of tranquillity. Built between 1839 and 1842, it's a beautiful place, and once the favourite landing point of Chinese sailors, before land reclamation pushed the sea far down the road. Curiously, the gates are Scottish and the tiles Dutch. (www. thianhockkeng.com.sg; 158 Telok Ayer St; ☉7.30am-5.30pm; Ⓜ Telok Ayer)

Singapore City Gallery   MUSEUM

5 ◎ Map p70, D4

See into Singapore's future at this interactive city-planning exhibition, which provides surprisingly compelling

Buddha Tooth Relic Temple

insight into the government's resolute policies of land reclamation, high-rise housing and meticulous urban planning. The highlight is an 11m-by-11m scale model of the central city, which shows just how different Singapore will look once all the projects currently under development join the skyline. (www.ura.gov.sg/gallery; URA Bldg, 45 Maxwell Rd; ⊙9am-5pm Mon-Sat; MⓂTanjong Pagar)

People's Park Complex SPA

6 ◉ Map p70, C1

The only reason to dive into this old-school Chinatown mall is for the cheap massage places ready to vie for your body parts (opt for the busier ones). Our favourite is **Mr Lim Foot Reflexology** (03-53 & 03-78, People's Park Complex;

30min foot reflexology $15; ⊙10am-11pm; MⓂChinatown), where your robust rub-down comes with televised local and Taiwanese soaps. (1 Park Rd; ⊙9am-11pm, individual stalls vary; MⓂChinatown)

Eating

Ding Dong SOUTHEAST ASIAN $$$

7 ✕ Map p70, E3

From the graphic bar tiles to the meticulous cocktails, to the wow-oh-wow modern takes on Southeast Asian flavours, it's all about attention to detail at this sucker-punch champ. Book a table and drool over zingtastic scallop ceviche with fresh coconut, sultry hay-smoked pork *bao* or tart-and-crunchy

Understand

Peranakan Culture

Peranakan heritage has been enjoying renewed interest, mainly triggered by *The Little Nonya*, a high-rating 2008 drama series focused on a Peranakan family, and the opening of Singapore's outstanding Peranakan Museum (p32). But who are the Peranakans?

Origins

In Singapore, Peranakan (locally born) people are the descendants of immigrants who married local, mostly Malay women. The largest Peranakan group in Singapore is the Straits Chinese. The men, called Babas, and the women, Nonya, primarily speak a patois that mixes Bahasa Malay, Hokkien dialect and English. The ancestors of the Straits Chinese were mainly traders from mainland China, their presence on the Malay peninsula stretching back to the Ming dynasty. The ancestors of Chitty Melaka and Jawi Peranakan were Indian traders, whose unions with local Malay women created their own unique traditions. All three groups are defined by an intriguing, hybrid culture created by centuries of cultural exchange and adaptation.

Weddings

No Peranakan tradition matches the scale of the traditional wedding. Originally spanning 12 days, its fusion of Fujian Chinese and Malay traditions included the consulting of a *sinseh pokwa* (astrologer) in the choosing of an auspicious wedding day, elaborate gifts delivered to the bride's parents in *bakul siah* (lacquered bamboo containers) and a young boy rolling across the bed three times in the hope for a male first-born. With the groom in Qing-dynasty scholar garb and the bride in a similarly embroidered gown and hat piece, the first day would include a tea ceremony. On the second day, the couple took their first meal together, feeding each other 12 dishes to symbolise the 12-day process, while the third day would see them offering tea to their parents and in-laws. On the *dua belah hari* (12th-day ceremony), the marriage was sealed and proof of the consummation confirmed with a discreet sighting of the stain on the bride's virginity handkerchief by the bride's parents and groom's mother.

red curry Wagyu short rib. Can't decide? Opt for the good-value 'Feed Me' menus. (www.dingdong.com.sg; 23 Ann Siang Rd; dishes $12-25, set menus $55 & $79; ⏱noon-2.30pm & 6-10.30pm Mon-Thu, noon-2.30pm & 6-11.30pm Fri, 6-11.30pm Sat)

Momma Kong's
SEAFOOD $$

8 🍴 Map p70, E2

Small, funky Momma Kong's is run by two young brothers and a cousin obsessed with crab. While the compact menu features numerous finger-licking, MSG-free crab classics, opt for the phenomenal chilli crab, its kick and non-gelatinous gravy unmatched in this town. One serve of crab and four giant, fresh *mantou* (steamed buns) should happily feed two stomachs. Unlike many other chilli crab joints, you'll find fixed prices and good-value combo deals. Book three days ahead. (📞6225 2722; www.momma-kongs.com; 34 Mosque St; mains from $20; ⏱5-10pm Tue-Sun; 🛜; Ⓜ Chinatown)

Lucha Loco
MEXICAN $$

9 🍴 Map p70, C4

Packed nightly with eye candy, flirtatious barkeeps and succulent Mexican street food, this pumping taquería-cum-garden-bar explodes with X-factor. While we adore the ceviche, tostaditas and addictive *elotes* (corn rolled in mayonnaise and Cotija cheese), it's the tacos, generously topped with fresh, beautiful produce, that leave us loco. No reservations, so head in early or late, or grab a Mezcal

and wait. (www.luchaloco.com; 15 Duxton Hill; dishes $8-20; ⏱4-10.15pm Tue-Thu, 4-11pm Fri, 6-11pm Sat; Ⓜ Outram Park, Tanjong Pagar)

Blue Ginger
PERANAKAN $$

10 🍴 Map p70, D5

Elegant Blue Ginger is one of the few places in Singapore showcasing the spicy, sour flavours of Peranakan food; a unique fusion of Chinese and Malay influences. Mouth-watering musts include *kueh pie tee* (shredded bamboo shoots and turnips garnished with shrimp in fried pie tee cups), *sambal terong goreng* (spicy fried eggplant) and a sublimely delicate Nonya fish head

Local Life
Pinnacle@Duxton

For killer city views at a bargain, head to the 50th-floor rooftop of **Pinnacle@Duxton** (Map p70, A5; www.pinnacleduxton.com.sg; Block 1G, 1 Cantonment Rd; admission $5; ⏱9am-10pm; Ⓜ Outram Park, Tanjong Pagar), the world's largest public housing complex. Skybridges connecting the seven towers provide a gob-smacking, 360-degree sweep of city, port and sea. Chilling out is encouraged, with patches of lawn, modular furniture and sunlounges. Payment is by EZ-Link card only (you can purchase one for $10 at the 7-Eleven store beside the ticket machine on level 1 of Block G). Rest the card on the ticket machine and $5 will be automatically deducted.

> **Understand**
> ## Temple Tales
>
> Before construction of the Thian Hock Keng Temple, the site was home to a much humbler joss house, where Chinese migrants would come to thank Mazu, the goddess of the sea, for their safe arrival. Their donations helped propel construction of the current temple, the low granite barrier of which once served to keep seawater out during high tide. Look up at the temple's ceiling in the right wing and you'll notice a statue of a man, seemingly lifting a beam. The statue is an ode to Indian migrants from nearby Chulia St, who helped construct the building. During restoration works in 1998, one of the roof beams revealed a surprising find – a scroll written by the Qing emperor Guangxu bestowing blessings on Singapore's Chinese community.

curry. (☎6222 3928; www.theblueginger.com; 97 Tanjong Pagar Rd; mains $12-38; �time noon-2.15pm & 6.30-9.45pm; Ⓜ Tanjong Pagar)

Maxwell Road Hawker Centre
HAWKER CENTRE $

11 ✕ Map p70, D4

One of Chinatown's most accessible hawker centres, Maxwell Road is a solid spot to savour some of the city's street-food staples. While stalls slip in and out of favour with Singapore's fickle diners, enduring favourites include **Tian Tian Hainanese Chicken Rice** (Stall 10), **Maxwell Fuzhou Oyster Cake** (Stall 5) and **Fried Sweet Potato Dumpling** (Stall 76). (cnr Maxwell & South Bridge Rds; dishes from $2.50; �time stalls vary; ✏; Ⓜ Chinatown)

Chinatown Complex
HAWKER CENTRE $

12 ✕ Map p70, C2

Leave Smith St's revamped 'Chinatown Food Street' to the out-of-

towners and join old-timers and foodies at this nearby labyrinth. The 25-minute wait for mixed claypot rice at **Lian He Ben Ji Claypot Rice** (Stall 02-198/199) is worth it, while the rich and nutty satay at **Shi Xiang Satay** (Stall 02-79) is insane. For a little TLC, opt for Ten Tonic Ginseng Chicken Soup at **Soup Master** (Stall 02-05). (11 New Bridge Rd; dishes from $2.50; �time individual stalls vary; Ⓜ Chinatown)

Sarnies
CAFE $$

13 ✕ Map p70, F3

Luscious, epic sarnies (British slang for sandwiches) bust the jaws of suits and hipsters at this new-school Aussie cafe. Farm-to-table produce shows off in sandwich combos like grilled aubergine and hummus, or blokey grass-fed steak with mushrooms and caramelised onions. Gourmet soups and salads pack an equal punch, while the weekend brunch includes house-cured bacon. Coffee snobs should sample the espresso martini. (📞6224 6091; www.sarniescafe.com; 136 Telok Ayer St; sandwiches & salads $13.50-16.50, weekend brunches $15.90-25.90; ⏱7.30am-9.30pm Mon-Fri, 9am-4pm Sat & Sun; Ⓜ Telok Ayer)

PS Cafe
INTERNATIONAL $$

14 🍴 Map p70, E3

From the ground-floor black marble bar to the upstairs sweep of crisp linen, Chesterfield banquettes and Dior-clad ladies, colonial glamour is always in vogue at this leafy, heavenly scented hideaway. Compare notes on husband and maid over vibrant, seductive bistro fare like the soy-cured salmon Big Nihon Salad or delicate miso cod. The popular weekend brunch cranks up the decadence, with free-flow Domaine Chandon or house wine options. *Cin cin, darlink*. (www.pscafe.com; 45 Ann Siang Rd; mains $19-36; ⏱restaurant 11.30am-10.30pm Mon-Fri, 9.30am-10.30pm Sat & Sun, bar open to 12.30am Mon-Thu & Sun, to 2am Fri & Sat; Ⓜ Chinatown)

Department of Caffeine
CAFE $$

15 🍴 Map p70, C4

The coffee cognoscenti don't just hang here for the smooth, nutty brews. They fill their bellies from an ever-changing menu of ridiculously fresh grub. Start the day with homemade granola, feel virtuous over chilli and garlic-spiked chargrilled broccoli, or fill up on comfort mains like succulent chicken with lemon sumac and za'atar. If you're feeling naughty, seek out the

honey and lavender tea cake. (DOC; 📞6223 3426; www.deptofcaffeine.com; 15 Duxton Rd; meals $15-18; ⏱10.30am-7.30pm Mon & Tue, 10.30am-10.30pm Thu & Fri, 9.30am-7.30pm Sat & Sun; Ⓜ Tanjong Pagar)

Ya Kun Kaya Toast
CAFE $

16 🍴 Map p70, F2

Though it's now part of a chain, this airy, retro coffeeshop is an institution, and the best way to start the day the Singaporean way. The speciality is buttery *kaya* (coconut jam) toast, dipped in runny egg (add black pepper and a few drops of soya sauce) and washed down with strong *kopi* (coffee). (www.yakun.com; 01-01 Far East Sq, 18 China St; kaya toast sets $4.20; ⏱7.30am-7pm Mon-Fri, 8.30am-5.30pm Sat & Sun; Ⓜ Telok Ayer)

Satay Street
HAWKER $

17 🍴 Map p70, H4

Each night, Boon Tat St is blocked to traffic and transformed into a KL-style sea of outdoor tables, beer-peddling aunties and little satay huts dubbed Satay Street. Order a few rounds of satay, some gravy-sopping rice cakes, a jug of Tiger, and feast on the cheap. You'll find it right behind the famous Lau Pa Sat hawker centre. (Boon Tat St; satay around $0.60 per stick; ⏱7pm-1am Mon-Fri, 3pm-1am Sat & Sun)

The Flying Squirrel
JAPANESE $$

18 🍴 Map p70, F3

This sneaky squirrel lurks down a laneway off Amoy St. Find it and your reward is fresh, delicious Japanese in a cool but cosy combo of brickwork, filament bulbs and designer chairs. Bento boxes are the lunchtime hit, while the more elaborate dinner menu includes a 're-invented' Wagyu Burger, in which bread and beef are minced together and pan-fried in a more-ish red wine sauce. Book ahead for dinner. (www.theflyingsquirrel.com.sg; 92 Amoy St, 01-02; lunches $16-38, dinner mains $13-36; ⏱11am-10pm Mon-Thu, to 11pm Fri & Sat; 🛜; Ⓜ Telok Ayer)

Tong Heng
BAKERY $

19 🍴 Map p70, D3

Hit the spot at this veteran pastry shop, specialising in pastries, tarts and cakes from the southern Chinese province of Guangdong. While locals rightfully flock here for the melt-in-your-mouth egg tarts, leave room for the slightly charred perfection of the *char siew su* (BBQ pork puff). Addictive personalities beware. (285 South Bridge Rd; snacks from $1.40; ⏱9am-10pm; Ⓜ Chinatown)

Ｑ Local Life
Everton Park HDB

The ground-floor space of Singapore's public housing blocks (HDBs) are usually scattered with gossipy uncles and aunties and shrieking kids. At Everton Park you're just as likely to find Third Wave coffee bloggers and design hunters. Top billing goes to **Nylon Coffee Roasters** (Map p70,B5; ☎6220 2330; www.nyloncoffee.sg; 4 Everton Park, 01-40; ⏱8.30am-5.30pm Mon & Wed-Fri, 9am-6pm Sat & Sun; Ⓜ Outram Park, Tanjong Pagar), a standing-room-only cafe-roastery. Buzzed up, pop into neighbouring **The Redundant Shop** (Map p70, A5; redundantshop.com; Everton Park, Block 5, 01-22A; ⏱11am-8pm Tue-Sat, to 5pm Sun; Ⓜ Outram Park, Tanjong Pagar), a catchment for design-literate curios from Singapore and beyond. Everton Park is 500m south of Outram Park MRT. Enter from Cantonment Rd, directly opposite the seven-tower Pinnacle@Duxton.

Drinking

Tippling Club
COCKTAIL BAR

20 🍸 Map p70, D4

Tippling Club propels mixology to dizzying heights, with a technique and creativity that could turn a teetotaler into a born-again soak. The best seats are at the bar, where under a ceiling of hanging bottles, passionate pros turn rare and precious spirits into wonders like the 'Smoky Old Bastard', a mellow concoction of whisky, sweet tobacco and citrus smoke. (☎6475 2217; www.tipplingclub.com; 38 Tanjong Pagar Rd; ⏱noon-midnight Mon-Fri, 6pm-midnight Sat)

Jekyll & Hyde
COCKTAIL BAR

21 🍸 Map p70, D5

By day a respectable nail salon, by night a killer cocktail lounge, Jekyll & Hyde splits itself into two distinct spaces – buzzing back bar and mild-mannered front space tailored for more tranquil tête-à-têtes. Whichever you choose, you'll be sipping on smooth, inspired libations like the Mr Bean, a strangely seductive blend of bean curd, vodka, kaya, butterscotch liqueur and Frangelico. (www.49tras.st; 49 Tras St; ⊘6pm-midnight Mon-Thu, 6pm-1am Fri & Sat; ⓜTanjong Pagar)

Jigger & Pony
COCKTAIL BAR

22 🍺 Map p70, F3

Once an art gallery, now a dark and slinky cocktail bar, Jigger & Pony is well known for honouring classic and long-forgotten libations. Japanese-style meticulousness steers the barkeeps, whose tricks include rare aperitivi like the crisp Cocchi Cooler (Cocchi Americano, soda water and flambéed orange peel) and one of the smoothest Negronis this side of Turin. (101 Amoy St; ⊘6pm-1am Mon-Thu, 6pm-3am Fri & Sat; ⓜTelok Ayer)

The Good Beer Company
BEER STALL

23 🍺 Map p70, C3

Injecting Chinatown Complex with a dose of new-school cool, this hawker-centre beer stall peddles an impressive booty of bottled craft suds, from homegrown Jungle to Belgian Trappistes Rochefort. A few stalls down is **Smith Street Taps** (11 New Bridge Rd, 02-062, Chinatown Complex; ⊘6.30-10.30pm Tue-Sat), run by a friendly dude and offering a rotating selection of craft and premium beers on tap. (11 New Bridge Rd,

FELIX HUG/GETTY IMAGES ©

Thian Hock Keng Temple (p72)

02-58, Chinatown Complex; ⊘6-10pm Mon-Sat; ⓜChinatown)

The Black Swan
BAR

24 🍺 Map p70, H2

Was that Rita Hayworth? You'll be mistaken for thinking so at this art deco marvel, set inside a former 1930s bank building. While we adore the bustling downstairs bar – complete with inlaid wood, geometric windows and centrepiece U-shaped bar – it's the upstairs Powder Room that takes the breath away – a dark, decadent, plush lounge perfect for top-tier whiskys or classic with-a-twist cocktails. (☎8181 3305; www.theblackswan.com.sg; 19 Cecil St; ⊘11am-1am Mon-Thu, to 2am Fri & Sat; ⓜRaffles Place)

GAVIN HELLIER/GETTY IMAGES ©

Pagoda St, Chinatown

Ô Batignolles WINE BAR

25 🚇 Map p70, F2

Don those Breton stripes and retreat to this corner bistro for a little joie de vivre. Run by a French couple and never short of unwinding lawyers and hopeless Francophiles, it's a fine choice for a well-priced glass (or bottle) of boutique wine, an *assiette de charcuterie* and a little Club St people-watching. (2 Gemmill Lane; ⊙noon-midnight Mon-Fri, 11am-midnight Sat, 11am-9pm Sun; 🛜; M Telok Ayer)

Breeze ROOFTOP BAR

26 🚇 Map p70, E3

For rooftop sipping without the raucous crowds, take the lift to this grown-up, seductive hideaway, perched above the Scarlet Hotel. Splashed with bold tropical fabrics and lush heliconia, it's a sensible spot for quiet conversations, romantic gazing or simply catching a late-night breeze while scanning a sea of rooftops and skyscrapers. (www.thescarlethotel.com; Scarlet Hotel, 33 Erskine Rd; ⊙5pm-1am Mon-Thu, to 2am Fri & Sat, to 11pm Sun; 🛜; M Chinatown)

1-Altitude ROOFTOP BAR

27 🚇 Map p70, H1

Extreme Altitude might be a better name for the world's highest alfresco bar, perched 282m above street level. Wedged across a triangle-shaped deck, its view of Singapore is unmatched, though the quality of the drinks fail to reach such lofty heights. Dress up (no shorts or open shoes, gents), snap away, then continue your evening at one of Singapore's better-quality drinking establishments. (www.1-altitude. com; 1 Raffles Pl, Level 63; admission $30, incl 1 drink; ⏱6pm-late; Ⓜ Raffles Place)

Drinks & Co   BAR

28 Ⓢ Map p70, E2

A crisp, contemporary bottle shop and bar in one, Drinks & Co showcases mostly New World wines and spirits, spanning both small- and larger-scale producers. It gets especially packed with post-work corporate types, who head in for well-priced bottles of plonk and pang-punching cheese platters and deli-style bites. Head in before the post-work rush or expect to wait for a seat. (drinksandco.asia; 44 Club St; ⏱2pm-midnight; Ⓜ Telok Ayer, Chinatown)

La Terrazza   BAR

29 Ⓢ Map p70, E3

The views across Chinatown and the CBD from this intimate rooftop bar, part of the hip Screening Room, are superb. Hunt down a comfy couch, kick off the shoes and have a shouting-into-each-other's-ears conversation over nostalgic '80s and '90s tunes. To reserve a bar table, call or email three days ahead. (☎6221 1694; www.screeningroom.com.sg; Level 4, 12 Ann Siang Rd; Ⓜ Chinatown)

Fry Bistro   ROOFTOP BAR

30 Ⓢ Map p70, E3

Unceremoniously stacked with beer cartons, DIY rooftop Fry flies under the radar with the Club St hordes. It's this very fact that makes it so appealing for a long lazy drinking session and (audible) late-night conversation. The vibe is chilled, the music good and the skyline view just as bewitching

Understand
Speaker's Corner

When Speakers' Corner hit Hong Lim Park in 2000, the government and (government-regulated) press hailed it as a step forward for Singaporean freedom of speech. Notorious sticklers for novelty, 400 Singaporeans took to the stand in the first month to address the crowds. A year later only 11 stepped up. Now, it's completely deserted and, cynics will say, an accurate symbol of the state of free speech in a country whose attitude towards politics is predominately apathetic. Of course, you're still free to step up and state your mind...as long as you're Singaporean, register in advance with local police, avoid blacklisted subjects such as religion, politics and ethnicity, and stay within Singapore's sedition laws. Still feel like speaking out?

✓ Top Tip

LGBT Singapore

Although public debate around LGBT (Lesbian, Gay, Bisexual and Transgender) rights is increasing, homosexual acts remain technically illegal. Despite this, a small but thriving LGBT scene exists, centred mostly on Neil Rd in Chinatown. Bars and clubs aside, annual events include the **Love & Pride Film Festival** (dates vary); June's **Pink Dot** (pinkdot.sg) solidarity gathering in Hong Lim Park and August pride festival **IndigNation** (www.plu.sg/indignation). For more info on what's on, check out www.travelgayasia.com, www.pluguide.com and www.utopia-asia.com.

as that from its louder, better-known neighbour. (☎8418 5995; www.facebook.com/FryBistro; 96B Club St; ⏱5pm-1am Mon-Wed, to 3am Thu-Sat; Ⓜ Chinatown)

Oxwell & Co   BAR

31 🚇 Map p70, E3

Laced with cockfighting posters, frontier-style benches and exposed copper pipes, it seems the only thing missing at jumping Oxwell & Co are some wagons out the front. What's not missing is a nightly crowd of tie-loosening suits downing lesser-known beers, solid wines and sophisticated grub such as graze-friendly marinated olives, and revamped Brit dude food like Yorkshire pudding. Up the

stairs, Gordon Ramsay protégé Mark Sargeant serves produce-driven modern British dishes; book the restaurant in advance. (www.oxwellandco.com; 5 Ann Siang Rd; ⏱10am-late Tue-Sat; Ⓜ Chinatown)

Yixing Xuan Teahouse   TEAHOUSE

32 🚇 Map p70, D4

Banker-turned-tea-purveyor Vincent Low is the man behind this venture, happily educating visitors about Chinese tea and the art of tea drinking. To immerse yourself more deeply, book a tea-ceremony demonstration with tastings ($20, 45 minutes). (www.yixingxuan-teahouse.com; 30/32 Tanjong Pagar Rd; ⏱10am-9pm Mon-Sat, to 7pm Sun; Ⓜ Tanjong Pagar)

Plain   CAFE

33 🚇 Map p70, C5

A high-cred combo of stark interiors, neatly piled design magazines and Scandi-style communal table, the Plain keeps hipsters purring with Australian Genovese coffee, decent all-day breakfasts (from $4) and sweet treats like lemon and lime tarts. Service is friendly and the vibe refreshingly relaxed. (www.theplain.com.sg; 50 Craig Rd; ⏱7.30am-5.30pm Mon-Fri, to 7.30pm Sat & Sun; Ⓜ Tanjong Pagar)

Tantric Bar   GAY

34 🚇 Map p70, C4

Two indoor bars and two alfresco palm-fringed courtyards is what you get at Singapore's best-loved gay drinking hole. Especially heaving on Friday and Saturday nights, it's a hit with preened locals and eager expats and out-of-towners, who schmooze and cruise to Kylie, Gaga and Katy Perry chart toppers. Lushes shouldn't miss Wednesday night, when $20 gets you two martinis. (78 Neil Rd; ⏱8pm-3am Sun-Fri, 8pm-4am Sat; Ⓜ Outram Park, Chinatown)

Entertainment

Chinese Theatre Circle   OPERA

35 ⭐ | Map p70, D3

Teahouse evenings organised by this nonprofit opera company are a wonderful, informal introduction to Chinese opera. Every Friday and Saturday at 8pm there is a brief talk on Chinese opera, followed by a 45-minute excerpt from an opera classic, performed by actors in full costume. You can also opt for a pre-show Chinese meal at 7pm. Book ahead. (☎6323 4862; www.ctcopera. com; 5 Smith St; show & snacks $25, show & dinner $40; ⏱7-9pm Fri & Sat; Ⓜ Chinatown)

Kyō   CLUB

36 ⭐ | Map p70, G3

From boring bank to thumping hotspot, this sprawling, Japanese-inspired playpen is home to the world's longest bar (expect the odd bar-top booty shake), suited eye-candy and sharp DJs spinning credible electro, house, funk or disco. If you're itching for a little midweek hedonism, you know where to go. (www.clubkyo.com; 133 Cecil St, B1-02,

Keck Seng Tower; ⏱9pm-3am Wed & Thu, to 5am Fri & Sat; Ⓜ Telok Ayer, Raffles Place)

Screening Room   CINEMA

37 ⭐ | Map p70, E3

If your idea of a good night involves sinking into a sofa and watching classic flicks, make some time for Screening Room. Expect anything from *On the Town* to *Sex, Lies and Videotape,* projected onto a pull-down screen. To watch a film, you'll need to spend a minimum of $15 on drinks or food at the cinema's Theatre Bar. (www.screeningroom.com.sg; 12 Ann Siang Rd; Ⓜ Chinatown, Telok Ayer)

Taboo   LGBT

38 ⭐ | Map p70, C4

After drinks at Tantric, cross the street and conquer the dance floor at what remains the favourite gay dance club in town. Expect the requisite line-up

---

◯ Local Life

Paper, Death & Sago Lane

The curious paper objects on sale around Chinatown – from miniature cars to computers – are offerings burned at funeral wakes to ensure the material wealth of the dead. Veteran **Nam's Supplies** (Map p70, D3; www.namsupplies.com; 22 Smith St; ⏱8am-7pm) has been peddling such offerings since 1948, when nearby Sago Lane heaved with so-called 'death houses', where dying relatives were sent to spend their final days.

of shirtless gyrators, doting straight women and regular racy themed nights. Note: only the chillout lounge is open on Wednesday and Thursday nights. (www.taboo.sg; 65 Neil Rd; ⏰8pm-2am Wed & Thu, 10pm-3am Fri, 10pm-4am Sat; Ⓜ Outram Park, Chinatown)

Shopping

Far East Legend
ANTIQUES, HANDICRAFTS

39 🔒 Map p70, E2

Slip inside this small, charmingly cluttered shop for an intriguing collection of furniture, lamps, handicrafts, statues and other objets d'art from all over Asia. You'll find anything from dainty porcelain snuff boxes to

ceramic busts of Chairman Mao. Best of all, the owner is usually willing to 'discuss the price'. (233 South Bridge Rd; ⏰11.30am-6.30pm; Ⓜ Chinatown)

Utterly Art
ART

40 🔒 Map p70, D2

Head upstairs to this tiny, welcoming gallery for works by contemporary Singaporean, Filipino and, on occasion, Cambodian artists. While painting is the gallery's main focus, exhibitions do dabble in sculpture and ceramics on occasion, with artworks priced from $50 to around $1400 (depending on the exhibition). Opening times can be a little erratic, so always call ahead if making the trip especially. (www.utterlyart.com.sg; Level 3, 20B Mosque St; ⏰varies, usually noon-8pm Mon-Sat, to 5.30pm Sun; Ⓜ Chinatown)

Willow & Huxley
FASHION, ACCESSORIES

41 🔒 Map p70, F3

Willow & Huxley peddles a sharp, vibrant edit of smaller independent labels like Australia's Finders Keepers and Bec & Bridge, Denmark's quirky Baum and Pferdgarten, and Sienna Miller's very own Twenty8Twelve. Jewellery spans vintage to statement, with a small selection of casual, beach-friendly threads for men courtesy of Australia's TCSS and New York's Onia and Psycho Bunny. (www.willowandhuxley.com; 20 Amoy St; ⏰9am-8pm Mon-Fri, 11am-3pm Sat; Ⓜ Telok Ayer)

> **⬭ Local Life**
>
> ### MAAD About Design
>
> Tap into Singapore's creative side at design flea market **MAAD** (Map p70, D4; Market of Artists and Designers; www.facebook.com/goMAAD; 28 Maxwell Rd). Held at the Red Dot Design Museum, it's a showcase for over 100 local artists and craftspeople, who sell anything and everything from handmade jewellery, totes and shoes to fashion, plush toys and postcards. The event is usually held from 5pm to midnight on one Friday night each month. Check the website for upcoming dates.

Eu Yan Sang

CHINESE MEDICINE

42 🔒 Map p70, E3

Get your *qi* back in order at Singapore's most famous and user-friendly Chinese medicine store. Pick up some Monkey Bezoar powder to relieve excess phlegm, or Liu Jun Zi pills to dispel dampness. You'll find herbal teas, soups and oils, and you can even consult a practitioner of Chinese medicine at the clinic next door (bring your passport). (www.euyansang.com.sg; 269 South Bridge Rd; ⏰shop 8.30am-7pm Mon-Sat, clinic 8.30am-6pm Mon, Tue, Thu & Fri, 9am-6pm Wed, 8.30am-7.30pm Sat; Ⓜ Chinatown)

Tong Mern Sern Antiques

ANTIQUES

43 🔒 Map p70, B5

An Aladdin's cave of dusty furniture, books, records, wood carvings, porcelain and other bits and bobs (we even found an old cash register), Tong Mern Sern is a curious hunting ground for Singapore nostalgia. A banner hung above the front door proclaims: 'We buy junk and sell antiques. Some fools buy. Some fools sell.' Better have your wits about you. (51 Craig Rd; ⏰9am-5.30pm Mon-Sat, 1.30-5.30pm Sun; Ⓜ Outram Park)

Yong Gallery

ANTIQUES

44 🔒 Map p70, D2

The owner here is a calligrapher, and much of his artwork is on sale. You'll also find jewellery, genuine jade products and antiques as well as more affordable gifts such as decorative book-

Night market, Pagoda St

marks, Chinese fans and clocks. It's fun browsing even if you're not in a buying mood. (260 South Bridge Rd; ⏰10am-7pm; Ⓜ Chinatown)

Yue Hwa Chinese Products

DEPARTMENT STORE

45 🔒 Map p70, D1

With a deco facade paging Shanghai, this six-storey department store specialises in all things Chinese. Downstairs you'll find medicine and herbs, clothes and cushions. Moving to Level 5, you'll pass through silks, food and tea, arts and crafts and household goods, before ending up in a large, cluttered sea of furniture. (www.yuehwa.com.sg; 70 Eu Tong Sen St; ⏰11am-9pm Sun-Fri, to 10pm Sat; Ⓜ Chinatown)

Local Life
Katong (Joo Chiat)

Getting There

M **MRT** Paya Lebar and Eunos stations are the closest stations.

🚌 **Bus** Routes 33 and 16 service Joo Chiat Rd.

Also known as Joo Chiat, Katong is the heart of Singapore's Peranakan community. It's an evocative mix of multicoloured shophouses, tucked-away temples and quaint workshops and handicraft studios, not to mention some of the city's best eateries. Try to head in during business hours, when locals hop in and out of heirloom shops in search of fabrics, produce and the next tasty snack.

❶ Geylang Serai Market

Geylang Serai Market (1 Geylang Serai; ⏱8am-10pm, individual stalls vary; Ⓜ Paya Lebar) packs in a lively wet market, hawker food centre and stalls selling everything from Malay CDs to skull-caps. If you're feeling peckish, hunt down some *pisang goreng* (banana fritters) and wash them down with a glass of *bandung* (milk with rose cordial syrup).

❷ Joo Chiat Road

Eclectic Joo Chiat Road is lined with dusty antiques workshops, Islamic fashion boutiques and low-fuss grocery shops. Detour left into Joo Chiat Tce to admire the Peranakan terraces at Nos 89 to 129, adorned with *pintu pagar* (swinging doors) and colourful ceramic tiles.

❸ Long Phuong

Head back to Joo Chiat Rd and continue south to **Long Phuong** (159 Joo Chiat Rd; dishes $6-22; ⏱11am-11pm; 🚌33, Ⓜ Eunos), a down-to-earth Vietnamese eatery serving up Singapore's best Vietnamese food. The *pho* (Vietnamese noodle soup) is simply gorgeous.

❹ Kuan Im Tng Temple

Fingers licked, it's a quick walk to **Kuan Im Tng Temple** (www.kuanimtng. org.sg; cnr Tembeling Rd & Joo Chiat Lane; ⏱5am-6.15pm; Ⓜ Paya Lebar), a Buddhist temple dedicated to Kuan Yin, goddess of mercy. Temple fans will appreciate the ornate roof ridges adorned with dancing dragons.

❺ Koon Seng Road Terraces

Koon Seng Rd is famous for its two rows of prewar, pastel-coloured Peranakan terraces, lavished with stucco dragons, birds, crabs and brilliant glazed tiles imported from Europe.

❻ Sri Senpaga Vinayagar Temple

One of Singapore's most beautiful Hindu temples, **Sri Senpaga Vinayagar Temple** (19 Ceylon Rd; ⏱6.30am-1.30pm & 6.30-9pm; 🚌10, 12, 14, 32, 40) features a *kamalapaatham*, a specially sculptured granite foot-stone found in certain ancient Hindu temples. The roof of the inner sanctum is covered in gold.

❼ Kim Choo Kueh Chang

Katong is stuffed with bakeries and dessert shops, but few equal old-school **Kim Choo Kueh Chang** (www.kimchoo. com; 109 East Coast Rd; ⏱10am-9.30pm; 🚌10, 14, 16, 32). Pick up traditional pineapple tarts and other Peranakan *kueh* (bite-sized snacks), and pit stop at the adjoining boutique for Peranakan ceramics and clothing.

❽ Katong Antique House

Tiny shop-cum-museum **Katong Antique House** (📞6345 8544; 208 East Coast Rd; ⏱11am-6.30pm by appointment only; 🚌10, 12, 14, 32, 40) is the domain of Peter Wee, a noted expert on Peranakan culture, and packed with his collection of books, Wantiques and cultural artefacts. By appointment only, though it's sometimes open to the public.

Local Life
Geylang

Getting There

🚌 **Bus** Routes 2, 13, 21, 26 and 51 run along Sims Ave through Geylang.

Ⓜ **MRT** Kallang, Aljunied and Paya Lebar are the closest stations.

Contradiction thrives in Geylang, a neighbourhood as famous for its shrines, temples and mosques as for its brothels and back-alley gambling dens. Head in for lunch, spend the afternoon wandering quaint *lorongs* (alleys), religious buildings and an under-the-radar gallery, then head back to neon-lit Geylang Rd for a long, lively evening of people-watching and unforgettably good local grub.

❶ Shi Sheng Frog Porridge

Geylang is famous for its frog porridge and the best place to try it is **Shi Sheng Frog Porridge** (235 Geylang Rd; ⏱11.45am-3.45am; 🚌2, 51, Ⓜ Kallang). Its Cantonese-style version is beautifully smooth and gooey, and only live frogs are used, ensuring that the meat is always fresh.

❷ Amitabha Buddhist Centre

Take a class on dharma and meditation at the seven-floor **Amitabha Buddhist Centre** (📞6745 8547; www.fpmtabc.org; 44 Lorong 25A; ⏱10.30am-6pm Tue-Sun; Ⓜ Aljunied); its upstairs meditation hall, swathed in red-and-gold cloth, is open to the public and filled with beautiful devotional objects. Check the website for class schedules.

❸ No Signboard Seafood

If you didn't brave the frog porridge, get messy over Singapore's best white-pepper crab at **No Signboard Seafood** (www.nosignboardseafood.com; 414 Geylang Rd; dishes from $15, crab per kg around $60; ⏱noon-1am; Ⓜ Aljunied). Madam Ong Kim Hoi started out with an unnamed hawker stall (hence 'No Signboard'), but the popularity of her seafood made her a rich woman, with six restaurants and counting.

❹ Lorong 24A

One alley worth strolling down is Lorong 24A, lined with renovated shophouses from which the sounds of chanting emerge. Many have been taken over by the numerous small

Buddhist associations in the area. Close by, tree-lined Lorong 27 is also worth a wander, jammed with colourful shrines and temples.

❺ Geylang Thian Huat Siang Joss Paper

Old-school **Geylang Thian Huat Siang Joss Paper** (503 Geylang Rd; ⏱8am-9.30pm; Ⓜ Aljunied) sells paper offerings used at funeral wakes. You'll find everything from giant cash registers, yachts and houses to lifelike shoes and piles of cash, all thrown into the fire to ensure a comfortable afterlife.

❻ Sri Sivan Temple

Built on Orchard Rd in the 1850s, the whimsically ornate **Sri Sivan Temple** (www.sstsingapore.com; 24, Geylang East Ave 2; ⏱6am-noon & 6-9pm) was uprooted and moved to Serangoon Rd in the 1980s before moving to its current location in 1993. The Hindu temple is especially unique for its fusion of North and South Indian architectural influences.

❼ Rochor Beancurd

End on a sweet note at **Rochor Beancurd** (745 Geylang Rd; dough sticks $1, bean curd from $1.20; ⏱24hr; 📷; Ⓜ Paya Lebar), a tiny bolthole with an epic reputation. People head here from all over the city for a bowl of its obscenely fresh, silky bean curd (opt for it warm). Order a side of dough sticks and dip to your heart's content. Oh, did we mention the egg tarts?

Local Life
Changi & Pulau Ubin

Getting There

🚌 **Bus** No 2 from Tanah Merah MRT reaches Changi Village. Bumboats (one way $2.50, bicycle surcharge $2; 6am to 9pm) connect Changi Village to Pulau Ubin.

Singapore's 'Far East' serves up a slower, nostalgic style of local life. Vests, Bermuda shorts and flip-flops are the look in chilled-out Changi Village, a place where out-of-towners are a less common sight. A short bumboat (motorised sampan) ride away, the rustic island of Pulau Ubin is the Singapore that development mercifully left behind.

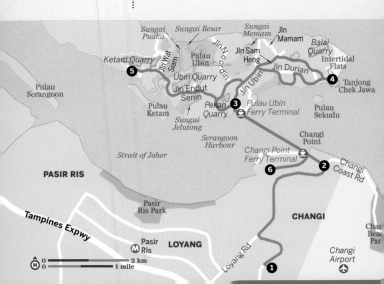

❶ Changi Museum & Chapel

Although no longer at the original Changi prison site, the **Changi Museum & Chapel** (☏6214 2451; www.changi museum.com; 1000 Upper Changi Rd N; admission free, audio guide adult/child $8/4, guided tour $12/8; ☉9.30am-5pm, last entry 4.30pm) remains a moving tribute to the Allied POWs captured, imprisoned and subjected to horrific treatment by the invading Japanese forces during WWII. Its centrepiece is a replica of the original Changi Chapel built by inmates.

❷ Changi Village

Hugging Singapore's far northeast coast, Changi Village is well worth a wander to experience a curiously relaxed side of Singapore. The vibe is almost village-like, and a browse around the area will turn up cheap clothes, batik, Indian textiles and electronics. Bumboats to Pulau Ubin depart from Changi Point Ferry Terminal, beside the bus terminal.

❸ Pulau Ubin Village

Your landing spot on Pulau Ubin is Pulau Ubin Village. Although not technically a tourist sight, its ramshackle nature channels a long-lost Singapore. If you're feeling peckish, turn left for a handful of eateries, mostly housed in *kampong* (village) huts. Tuck into noodles, rice dishes or seafood staples like chilli crab (expect to pay around $20 per person for the latter). The village is also the place to rent bikes; day rentals cost around $5 to $12.

❹ Chek Jawa Wetlands

If you only have time for one part of Pulau Ubin, make it **Chek Jawa Wetlands** (admission free; ☉8.30am-6pm). Located at the island's eastern end, its 1km coastal boardwalk juts out into the sea before looping back through protected mangrove swamp to the 20m-high Jejawi Tower, offering a stunning panorama. You can't bring your bike into the reserve so make sure you rent one that comes with a bike lock.

❺ German Girl Shrine

Housed in a yellow hut beside an Assam tree, the German Girl Shrine is one of the island's quirkier sights. Legend has it that the young German daughter of a coffee plantation manager was running away from British troops who had come to arrest her parents during WWI and fell fatally into the quarry behind her house. Somewhere along the way, this daughter of a Roman Catholic family became a Taoist deity, whose help some Chinese believers seek for good health and fortune.

❻ Coastal Settlement

Back in Changi, end the day at **Coastal Settlement** (☏6475 0200; www.thecoastal settlement.com; 200 Netheravon Rd; mains $16-24, pizzas $21-23; ☉10.30am-midnight Tue-Sun, last food orders 9.30pm; ☐29), an eclectic bar-lounge-restaurant pimped with retro objects and set in a black-and-white colonial bungalow on lush, verdant grounds.

Explore

Little India & Kampong Glam

Little India bursts with vibrancy. This is a world where goods crowd the five-foot-ways, shophouses are the colour of crayons and men in *dhotis* (loincloth) gossip over authentic *dosa* (savoury pancakes) at the marketplace. Walk 15 minutes southeast and you're in calmer Kampong Glam, dubbed Arab St. Head here for beautiful mosques, colourful fabrics, trendy boutiques and delicious grub.

The Sights in a Day

☀ Breakfast south Indian style at **Ananda Bhavan** (p104) then head north along colourful Serangoon Rd until you hit Hindu showpiece **Sri Veeramakaliamman Temple** (p98). Continue north to **Sri Srinivasa Perumal Temple** (p98), or go as far as bargain mecca **Mustafa Centre** (p111) and dive in for cut-price electronics, threads, shoes and jewellery.

☀ Recharge with Indian home-cooking at **Lagnaa Barefoot Dining** (p101), drop into the reputedly lucky **Kuan Im Thong Hood Cho Temple** (p100), then bargain hunt at **Bugis Street Market** (p110). Next stop: Kampong Glam. If you're not shopped out, pick up a bespoke fragrance at **Sifr Aromatics** (p109) and hit fashion-literate **Haji Lane** (p111), otherwise head straight to whimsical **Sultan Mosque** (p99).

☾ Come dinner, dig into real-deal Italian at fashionable **Cicheti** (p103) or keep it local with *murtabak* (stuffed savoury pancake) at no-frills classic **Zam Zam** (p105). Down made-to-measure cocktails at **Bar Stories** (p106), people watch at buzzing **Piedra Negra** (p107) or live tunes at boho **BluJaz Café** (p108).

For a local's day in Little India, see p94.

🔍 Local Life

A Stroll in Little India (p94)

♥ Best of Singapore

Food
Lagnaa Barefoot Dining (p101)

Cicheti (p103)

Zam Zam (p105)

Nan Hwa Chong Fish-Head Steamboat Corner (p104)

Drinking
BluJaz Café (p108)

Maison Ikkoku (p106)

Artistry (p106)

Shopping
Sifr Aromatics (p109)

Little Shophouse (p109)

Getting There

Ⓜ **MRT** Little India is on the Purple Line. For Kampong Glam, walk 300m from Bugis (Green and Blue Lines).

Ⓜ **Metro** Farrer Park (Purple Line) is handy for the north end of Little India and Mustafa Centre.

Local Life
A Stroll in Little India

Loud, colourful and refreshingly raffish, Little India stands in contrast to the more staid parts of the city. Dive into a gritty, pungent wonderland of dusty grocery shops, gold and sari traders, haggling Indian families and heady Hindu temples. Jumble them all together with a gut-busting booty of fiery eateries and you have Singapore's most hypnotic, electrifying urban experience.

1 Buffalo Road

Plunge into subcontinental Singapore on Buffalo Rd. It's a bustling strip packed with brightly coloured facades, Indian produce shops, Hindu shrines and garland stalls. Flowers used to make the garlands are highly symbolic: both the lotus and white jasmine spell purity, while the yellow marigold denotes peace.

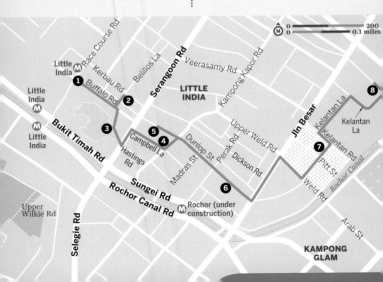

❷ Tan House

As you walk up Buffalo Rd towards Serangoon Rd, look for an alley leading to Kerbau Rd on your left. Take a quick detour down it to be dazzled by Tan House. Sitting on the corner of the alley and Kerbau Rd, this is quite possibly Singapore's most colourful building. Once you've picked up your jaw, head back onto Buffalo Rd.

❸ Tekka Centre Wet Market

If it's morning, slip into **Tekka Centre Wet Market** (cnr Serangoon & Buffalo Rds; ⏱6am-1.30pm), where locals battle it out for the city's freshest produce. It's an intense place, stocking everything from fresh yoghurt and dried curry spices to bitter gourds, black-skin chicken and halal meats. If you're after a sari, the top floor has an army of vendors.

❹ Indian Heritage Centre

Opening in 2015, the $12 million **Indian Heritage Centre** (www.indian-heritage.org.sg; cnr Campbell Ln & Clive St; Ⓜ Little India) explores the origins and heritage of Singapore's Indian community through artefacts, maps, archival footage and multimedia. The building itself is a striking contemporary statement. Iridescent during the day, its translucent facade becomes transparent at night, revealing a suitably colour-packed mural.

❺ Thandapani Co

Slip into Dunlop St and look for **Thandapani Co** (124 Dunlop St). Adorned with hessian bags packed with chillies, fennel seeds and other Indian staples, this grocery shop is considered one of the city's best spice vendors, stocking ingredients you won't find elsewhere.

❻ Abdul Gafoor Mosque

Equally enticing is **Abdul Gafoor Mosque** (41 Dunlop St; Ⓜ Little India), with its intriguing mix of Islamic and Victorian architecture. Completed in 1910, it features an elaborate sundial crowning its main entrance, each of its 25 rays decorated with Arabic calligraphy denoting the names of 25 prophets.

❼ Sungei Road Thieves Market

A ramshackle collection of tarpaulins and random junk, **Sungei Road Thieves Market** (Sungei Rd, Weld Rd, Pasar Lane & Pitt St; ⏱afternoons; Ⓜ Bugis) offers a glimpse into the city's underbelly. Amid the sea of dusty laptops, cassette tapes and worn stilettos, you may just find a true gem, from Chairman Mao dinner plates to a Mont Blanc pen.

❽ Sungei Road Laksa

End your local experience with a cheap, steamy fix at **Sungei Road Laksa** (Block 27, Jalan Berseh #01-100, Jin Shui Kopitiam; laksa $2; ⏱9am-6pm, closed 1st & 3rd Wed of month). The fragrant, savoury coconut-base soup enjoys a cult following, and only charcoal is used to keep the precious gravy warm. To avoid the lunchtime crowds, head in before 11.30am or after 2pm.

Lavender St

Foch Rd

Horne Rd

Tyrwhitt Rd

Jln Besar Stadium

King George's Ave

Jln Besar

Sturdee Rd

Beatty Rd

Petain Rd

Plumer Rd

Kitchener Rd

Townshend Rd

Sri Vadapathira Kaliamman Temple

D **3** ⊙

Maude Rd

Serangoon Rd

Leong San **4** ⊙
See Temple

Sakya Muni **5** ⊙
Buddha Gaya
Temple

Sam Leong Rd

Syed Alwi Rd

31 ☾

2 ⊙
Sri Srinivasa
Perumal
Temple

Verdun Rd

Rowell Rd

Hindoo Rd

Tessensohn Rd

Race Course Rd

43 🛏

Kampong Kapor Rd

Desker Rd

16 ✕

Baboo La

Hindoo Rd

Rangoon Rd

🅜 Farrer
Park

Owen Rd

Burmah Rd

Norris Rd

Birch Rd

Roberts La

Kinta Rd

Race Course La

Baboo La

Owen Rd

Klang Rd

**LITTLE
INDIA**

Sri **1** ⊙
Veeramakaliamman
Temple

Bellios La

Veerasamy Rd

Northumberland Rd

Race Course Rd

Chander Rd

Hampshire Rd

22 ✕

17 ✕

Ketbau Rd

Farrer
Park
Fields

Little 🅜
India

🕉 **35**

Buffalo Rd

Dorset Rd

A **B** **C** **D** **E**

1 **2** **3** **4**

🅝

400 m
0.25 miles

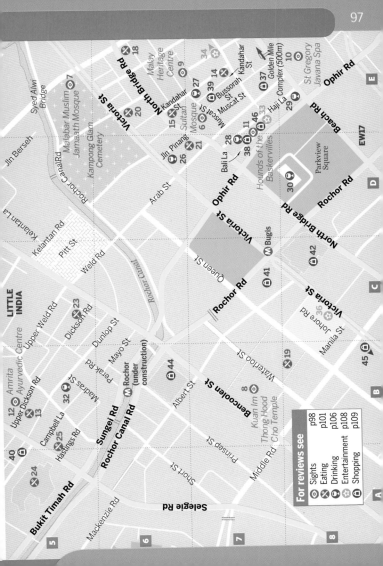

LITTLE INDIA

Syed Alwi Bridge

Malabar Muslim Jamaath Mosque 🔘 7

Kampong Glam Cemetery

Jln Berseh

Rochor Canal Rd

Victoria St

North Bridge Rd

Malay Heritage Centre

✖ 18

🏠 9

🌀 34

Kandahar St

Kelantan La

Pitt St

Weld Rd

Kelantan Rd

Dunlop St

Upper Weld Rd

🏠 23

Dickson Rd

Madras St

Perak Rd

Mayo St

Rochor (under construction) Ⓜ

🏠 44

Albert St

Rochor Canal Rd

Sungei Rd

Campbell La

🏠 25

Hastings Rd

Bukit Timah Rd

✖ 24

🏠 40

Amrita Ayurvedic Centre

🔘 12

Upper Dickson Rd

✖ 13

✖ 32

Prinsep St

Short St

Mackenzie Rd

Selegie Rd

15 ✖ St

🔘 20

Jln Pinang

🏠 26

🔘 21

Sultan Mosque 🔘 6

Muscat St

🏠 27

🏠 39 14

Bussorah St

Muscat St

Bali La

🏠 28

38 🏠

🏠 11 🏠 46

🌀 33

Kandahar St

🏠 37

Golden Mile Complex (500m)

Haji La

🏠 29

St Gregory Javana Spa

Ophir Rd

Beach Rd

Arab St

Ophir Rd

Victoria St

Hounds of the Baskervilles

🏠 30

Parkview Square

Rochor Rd

EW17

Beach Rd

North Bridge Rd

Rochor Rd

Queen St

Ⓜ Bugis

🏠 41

🏠 42

Victoria St

Johore Rd

🏠 36

Manila St

Rochor Rd

✖ 19

Waterloo St

Kuan Im Thong Hood Cho Temple 🔘 8

Bencoolen St

Middle Rd

🏠 45

For reviews see

🔘	Sights	p98
✖	Eating	p101
🍷	Drinking	p106
🎭	Entertainment	p108
🏠	Shopping	p109

A   B   C   D   E

5   6   7   8

Sights

Sri Veeramakaliamman Temple
HINDU TEMPLE

1 ○ Map p96, B4

Little India's most colourful, bustling temple is dedicated to the ferocious goddess Kali, depicted wearing a garland of skulls, ripping out the insides of her victims and sharing more tranquil family moments with her sons Ganesh and Murugan. The blood-thirsty consort of Shiva has always been popular in Bengal, the birthplace of the labourers who built the structure in 1881. The temple is at its most evocative during each of the four daily *puja* (prayer) sessions. (141 Serangoon Rd; ○5.15am-12.15pm & 4-9.15pm; M Little India)

Sri Srinivasa Perumal Temple
HINDU TEMPLE

2 ○ Map p96, D2

This temple dedicated to Vishnu dates from 1855, though the striking, 20m-tall *gopuram* (tower) is a $300,000 1966 add-on. Inside is a statue of Vishnu, his sidekicks Lakshmi and Andal, and his bird-mount Garuda. The temple is the starting point for a colourful, wince-inducing street parade during the Thaipusam festival. (397 Serangoon Rd; ○5.45am-noon & 5-9pm; M Farrer Park)

Sri Vadapathira Kaliamman Temple
HINDU TEMPLE

3 ○ Map p96, D1

Dedicated to Kaliamman, the Destroyer of Evil, this South Indian temple began life in 1870 as a modest shrine, but underwent a significant facelift in 1969 to transform it into the beauty standing today. The carvings here – particularly on the domed *vimana* inside – are among the best temple artwork you'll see anywhere in Singapore. (555 Serangoon Rd; ○6am-noon & 4.30-9pm Sun-Thu, 6am-12.30pm & 4.30-9.30pm Fri & Sat; M Farrer Park, Boon Keng)

Leong San See Temple
BUDDHIST TEMPLE

4 ○ Map p96, D1

Dating from 1917 and dedicated to Kuan Yin (Guanyin), this relatively modest temple often swells with more religious fervour than many larger Buddhist temples in Singapore. The name translates as Dragon Mountain Temple and its tiled roof ridge is decorated with animated chimera, dragons, flowers and human figures. To get here, walk north up Serangoon Rd then, opposite Beatty Rd, turn left through a decorative archway emblazoned with the Chinese characters for the temple (龍山寺) and you'll find it at the end of the lane. (371 Race Course Rd; ○7.30am-5pm; M Farrer Park)

ROBIN BUSH/GETTY IMAGES ©

Sri Veeramakaliamman Temple

Sakya Muni Buddha Gaya Temple

BUDDHIST TEMPLE

5 ◉ Map p96, D1

Dominating this temple, also known as the Temple of 1000 Lights, is a 15m-tall, 300-tonne Buddha. Keeping him company is an eclectic cast of deities, including Kuan Yin, the Chinese goddess of mercy and, interestingly, the Hindu deities Brahma and Ganesh. The yellow tigers flanking the entrance symbolise protection and vitality, while the huge mother-of-pearl Buddha footprint to your left as you enter is reputedly a replica of the footprint on top of Adam's Peak in Sri Lanka. (Temple of 1000 Lights; 366 Race Course Rd; ⊙8am-4.30pm; Ⓜ Farrer Park)

Sultan Mosque

MOSQUE

6 ◉ Map p96, E7

Seemingly pulled from the pages of the *Arabian Nights,* Singapore's largest mosque is nothing short of enchanting, designed in the Saracenic style and topped by a golden dome. It was originally built in 1825 with the aid of a grant from Raffles and the East India Company, after Raffles' treaty with the Sultan of Singapore allowed the Malay leader to retain sovereignty over the area. In 1928, the original mosque was replaced by the present magnificent building, designed by an Irish architect. (www.sultanmosque.org.sg; 3 Muscat St; ⊙9am-noon & 2-4pm Sat-Thu, 2.30-4pm Fri; Ⓜ Bugis)

Malabar Muslim Jama-ath Mosque
MOSQUE

7 ◉ Map p96, E5

Architecture goes easy-wipe at the golden-domed Malabar Muslim Jama-Ath Mosque, a curious creation clad entirely in striking, blue geometric tiles. This is the only mosque on the island dedicated to Malabar Muslims from the South Indian state of Kerala, and though the building was commenced in 1956, it wasn't officially opened until 1963 due to cash-flow problems. This 'better late than never' motif continues with the tiling, only completed in 1995. (www.malabar.org.sg; 471 Victoria St; ⊙2.30-4pm & 5-6.30pm; Ⓜ Lavender)

◯ Local Life
Banksy, Asian-Style
Street artist Ernest Zacharevic (www.zachas.com) has been dubbed the Malaysian Banksy. Born in Lithuania and based in Penang, the 20-something artist has garnered a global following for his fantastically playful, interactive street art. Zacharevic's murals often incorporate real-life props, whether old bicycles, chairs, even the moss growing out of cracks. In one small work opposite the Malabar Muslim Jama-ath Mosque, two exhilarated kids freewheel it on a pair of 3D supermarket trolleys. To the right, a young boy somersaults out of a box, while further south on the corner of Victoria St and Jln Pisang, a giant girl caresses a lion cub.

Kuan Im Thong Hood Cho Temple
BUDDHIST TEMPLE

8 ◉ Map p96, B7

Awash with the frenetic click of Chinese divination sticks, this is one of Singapore's busiest (and according to devotees, luckiest) temples. It's dedicated to the goddess of mercy Kuan Yin, a much-loved peddler of good fortune. Flower sellers and fortune tellers swarm around the entrance, while further up the street, believers rub the belly of a large bronze Buddha Maitreya for extra luck. Pragmatic worshippers also offer prayers at the polychromatic **Sri Krishnan Hindu Temple** (152 Waterloo St) next door. (178 Waterloo St; ⊙6am-6.30pm; Ⓜ Bugis)

Malay Heritage Centre
MUSEUM

9 ◉ Map p96, E6

The Kampong Glam area is the historic seat of Malay royalty, resident here before the arrival of Raffles, and the *istana* (palace) on this site was built for the last sultan of Singapore, Ali Iskander Shah, between 1836 and 1843. It's now a museum, with recently revamped galleries exploring Malay-Singaporean culture and history, from the early migration of traders to Kampong Gelam, to the development of Malay-Singaporean film, theatre, music and publishing. (✆6391 0450; www.malayheritage.org.sg; 85 Sultan Gate; adult/under 6yr $4/free; ⊙10am-6pm Tue-Sun; Ⓜ Bugis)

St Gregory Javana Spa
SPA

10 ⊙ Map p96, E8

St Gregory's is a major player in the relaxation stakes, with four facilities in Singapore. This recently refurbished branch is at the Parkroyal on Beach Rd, its forest-inspired design a dreamy backdrop for treatments ranging from Swedish massage, wraps and milk baths, to traditional Chinese therapies and oil-based Ayurvedic massage. (☑6505 5755; www.stgregoryspa.com; 7500 Beach Rd, Level 4, The Parkroyal; treatments $40-300; ☺10am-10pm Mon-Fri, 9am-9pm Sat & Sun; ⓜBugis, Nicoll Highway)

Hounds of the Baskervilles
BARBER, TATTOO PARLOUR

11 ⊙ Map p96, E7

Inked hipsters, antique cabinets bursting with clippers and a hissing espresso machine: no place screams new-school Singapore like this old-school-inspired barber-cum-tattoo parlour. Get clippered or snipped (walk-ins only), or pimp your skin with a striking new tatt. The top dog artist here is Rosman, a Javanese dude famed for his batik designs. (☑6299 1197; 24 Bali Lane; buzz cuts/full cuts/shaves $15/38/35; ☺11am-10pm Mon-Sat; ⓜBugis)

Amrita Ayurvedic Centre
MASSAGE

12 ⊙ Map p96, B5

If Little India's hyperactive energy leaves you frazzled, revive the Indian way with an Ayurvedic (traditional Indian medicine) massage at this

Sultan Mosque (p99)

modest, friendly massage joint. Treatments include Udvarthanam (using a paste of herbs and grains to cleanse the skin and improve circulation) and the highly popular Abhyangam (synchronised massage using medicated oils). (☑6299 0642; www.amrita.com.sg; 11 Upper Dickson Rd; 30min massages from $35; ☺9am-9pm Mon-Sat, 8am-3pm Sun; ⓜLittle India)

Eating

Lagnaa Barefoot Dining
INDIAN $$

13 ✗ Map p96, B5

You can choose your level of spice at friendly Lagnaa: Level 3 denotes standard spiciness, Level 4 significant

Understand

The Singaporean Table

Food is one of Singapore's greatest drawcards, the nation's melting pot of cultures creating one of the world's most diverse, drool-inducing culinary landscapes.

Chinese

Thank the Hainanese for Hainanese chicken rice (steamed fowl and rice cooked in chicken stock, served with a clear soup and a chilli-ginger dip), and the Hokkiens for *hokkien mee* (yellow Hokkien noodles with prawns) and *char kway teow* (stir-fried noodles with cockles, Chinese sausage and dark sauce). Teochew cuisine is famed for its rice porridge, while Cantonese classics include *won ton* soup.

Malaysian & Indonesian

Feast on Katong laksa (spicy coconut curry broth with noodles, prawns, cockles, fish cake, bean sprouts and laksa leaf), *ikan assam* (fried fish in a sour tamarind curry) and *nasi lemak* (coconut rice with fried fish and peanuts). Equally mouth-watering is *nasi padang*, which sees steamed rice paired with a choice of meat and vegetable dishes like *sambal tofu-tempeh* (spicy tofu and fermented beans).

Peranakan

Peranakan (Nonya) food is a cross-cultural fusion of Chinese and Malay influences. Dishes are tangy, spicy and commonly flavoured with chillies, shallots, *belacan* (Malay fermented prawn paste), preserved soya beans, peanuts, coconut milk and galangal (a ginger-like root). Classics include *otak otak* (a sausage-like blend of fish, coconut milk, chilli paste, galangal and herbs grilled in a banana leaf).

Indian

South India's hot flavours dominate. Tuck into thali (rice plate), a combination of rice, vegetable curries, *rasam* (hot, sour soup) and dessert served on a large banana leaf. Leave room for *roti prata* (fried flat bread served with a curry sauce), *masala dosa* (thin pancake filled with spiced potatoes and chutney) and halal (Muslim) *murtabak* (lightly grilled dough stuffed with onion and seasoned meat, usually mutton).

spiciness and anything above admirable bravery. Whatever level you opt for, you're in for finger-licking good homestyle cooking from both ends of Mother India, devoured at either Western seating downstairs or on floor cushions upstairs. Indecisive? Order chef Kaesavan's famous Threadfin fish curry. (☑6296 1215; www.lagnaa.com; 6 Upper Dickson Rd; dishes $6-20; ☺11.30am-10pm; ☏; Ⓜ Little India)

Cicheti
ITALIAN $$

14 Ⓧ Map p96, E7

Cool-kid Cicheti is a slick, friendly, buzzing scene of young-gun pizzaioli, trendy diners and seductive, contemporary Italian dishes made with hand-picked market produce. Tuck into beautifully charred wood-fired pizzas, made-from-scratch pasta and evening standouts like *polpette di carne grana* (slow-cooked meatballs topped with shaved Grana Padana). Book early in the week if heading there on a Friday or Saturday night. (☑6292 5012; www.cicheti.com; 52 Kandahar St; pizzas $17-25, mains $25-38; ☺noon-3pm & 6.30-11pm Mon-Fri, 6.30-11pm Sat; Ⓜ Bugis)

Warong Nasi Pariaman
MALAYSIAN, INDONESIAN $

15 Ⓧ Map p96, E6

It might not be much to look at, but this corner *nasi padang* stall is the stuff of legend. Do not miss the *belado* (fried mackerel in a slow-cooked chilli, onion and vinegar sauce), delicate *rendang* beef or *ayam bakar* (grilled chicken with coconut sauce). Get here by 11am to avoid the hordes. And be warned: most of it sells out by 1pm. (☑6292 2374; 738 North Bridge Rd; dishes $2.60-5; ☺7.30am-2.30pm Mon-Sat; Ⓜ Bugis)

Sankranti
INDIAN $

16 Ⓧ Map p96, C3

Arguably the best of a cluster of good restaurants in and around Little India's 24-hour shopping hub, the Mustafa Centre, Sankrati serves specialities from the South Indian state of Andhra Pradesh. The extensive menu also includes a number of North Indian dishes and has an enticing choice of set-meal thalis. The pick of the bunch is the Sankranti Special, a 10-piece culinary extravaganza. (100 Sayed Alwi Rd; mains from $8; ☺11.30am-4pm & 6pm-midnight Mon-Thu, 11.30am-midnight Fri-Sun; Ⓜ Little India)

Gandhi Restaurant
SOUTH INDIAN $

17 Ⓧ Map p96, A4

It may be a canteen-style joint with shabby service and cheap decor, but who cares when the food is this good? Wash your hands at the sink at the back and tuck into delicious set-meal thali, *dosa* (paper-thin lentil-flour pancake) or *uttapam* (thick, savoury South Indian rice pancake with finely chopped onions, green chillies, coriander and coconut). (29 Chander Rd; dishes from $2, set meals from $4; ☺11am-11pm; Ⓜ Little India)

ANDREW ROWAT/GETTY IMAGES ©

Late-night dining, Little India

Nan Hwa Chong Fish-Head Steamboat Corner   CHINESE $$

18 Map p96, E6

If you only try fish-head hotpot once, do it at this noisy, open-fronted veteran. Cooked on charcoal, the large pot of fish head is brought to you in steaming, *tee po* (dried flat sole fish) spiked broth. One pot is enough for three or four people, and can stretch to more with rice and side dishes. (812-816 North Bridge Rd; fish steamboats around $20; 4.30pm-12.30am; M Lavender)

Ananda Bhavan   INDIAN, VEGETARIAN $

You will find this super-cheap chain restaurant near the Tekka Centre (see

24 Map p96, A5). It is a top spot to sample South Indian breakfast staples like *idly* and *dosa* (spelt 'thosai' on the menu). It also does great-value thali, some of which are served on banana leaves. You'll find other Little India outlets at 58 Serangoon Rd and 95 Syed Alwi Rd, as well as an outlet at Changi Airport's Terminal 2. (www.anandabhavan.com; Block 663, 01-10 Buffalo Rd; set meals $6-9; 7am-10.30pm; M Little India)

QS269 Food House   HAWKER $

19 Map p96, B8

This is not so much a 'food house' as a loud, crowded undercover laneway lined with cult-status food stalls. Work up a sweat with a bowl of award-winning coconut curry noodle soup from **Ah Heng Curry Chicken Bee Hoon Mee** (Stall 01-236; dishes from $4; ⏱8am-5pm Sat-Thu) or join the queue at the equally cultish **New Rong Liang Ge Cantonese Roast Duck Boiled Soup** (Stall 01-235; dishes from $2.50; ⏱7am-8pm), with succulent roast duck dishes that draw foodies from across the city. (Block 269b Queen St; ⏱individual stalls vary; Ⓜ Bugis)

Symmetry   CAFE $$

20 🍴 Map p96, E6

With its clutter of rusty beams, random lamps and indie tunes, Symmetry feels like a garage made for band jams. But it's all about the grub, coffee and suds. Book ahead for the weekend brunch, its wickedly good offerings including wild mushroom duxelle beignets, pork collar-stuffed croissants and a satisfying Eggs Sur Le Plat (with pork sausage, smoked paprika, cherry tomato coulis and creamed baby spinach). (www.symmetry.com.sg; 9 Jalan Kubor; brunch $16-24; ⏱10.30am-9pm Mon, to 11pm Tue-Thu, to midnight Fri, 9am-midnight Sat, 9am-9pm Sun; 📶; Ⓜ Bugis)

Zam Zam   MALAYSIAN $

21 🍴 Map p96, D7

These guys have been here since 1908 so they know what they're doing. Tenure hasn't bred complacency, though. The touts still try to herd customers in off the street while frenetic chefs inside whip up delicious *murtabak,* the restaurant's speciality savoury pancakes,

filled with succulent mutton, chicken, beef, venison or even sardines. (699 North Bridge Rd; murtabak from $5, dishes $6-20; ⏱7am-11pm; 📶; Ⓜ Bugis)

Jaggi's   INDIAN PUNJABI $

22 🍴 Map p96, A4

One of the few authentic, no-nonsense outfits in a string of otherwise touristy, overpriced Indian restaurants on Race Course Rd, canteen-style Jaggi's peddles delicious Punjabi food to loyal locals. Point and choose and mix and match until you have a meal's worth of dishes, then pay the boss and take your tray of goodies to your table. (34-36 Race Course Rd; dishes $2.50-$5; ⏱11.30am-3.30pm & 5.30-10.30pm Mon-Thu, to 10.45pm Fri, 11am-4pm & 5.30-10.45pm Sat & Sun; 🖊; Ⓜ Little India)

Cocotte   FRENCH $$$

23 🍴 Map p96, C5

Never mind the Little India address, hip Cocotte is red, white and blue down to its succulent French *jus.* Plan your next Gallic adventure over garlicky *gougères aux escargots* (snails wrapped in cheese pastry), tender pork, veal and sage *crépinettes,* or the signature *poulet rôti,* a whole chicken roasted to perfection and served with seasonal vegetables and rich pan juices. (📞6298 1188; www.restaurantcocotte.com; 2 Dickson Rd, Wanderlust; mains from $34; ⏱noon-2pm & 6-9.30pm Sun, Mon, Wed & Thu, noon-2.30pm & 6-10pm Fri & Sat; Ⓜ Little India, Bugis)

Tekka Centre
HAWKER CENTRE $

24 Map p96, A5

Queue up for biryani, *dosai* (South Indian savoury pancake), *roti prata* (fried flat bread served with a curry sauce) and *teh tarik* (pulled tea), then wedge yourself into a table at this legendary hawker centre wrapped around the sloshed guts and hacked bones of the wet market. (cnr Serangoon & Buffalo Rds; dishes $2-10; ⏱7am-11pm; ⚲; Ⓜ Little India)

Moghul Sweet Shop
SWEETS $

25 Map p96, B5

If you're after a subcontinental sugar rush, tiny Moghul is the place to get it. Sink your teeth into luscious *gulab jamun* (syrup-soaked fried dough balls), harder-to-find *rasmalai* (paneer cheese soaked in cardamom-infused clotted cream) and *barfi* (condensed milk and sugar slice) in flavours such as pistachio, chocolate and...carrot. (48 Serangoon Rd; sweets from $1; ⏱9.30am-9.30pm; Ⓜ Little India)

Drinking

Artistry
CAFE

26 Map p96, D6

Killer coffee, rotating art exhibitions and frequent after-hours events, ranging from live music and dance to themed cocktail soirees. Artistry is a hipster version of the cultural salon. Swig on interesting artisanal beers and ciders, or tuck into fresh, delicious grub (served till 5pm) like the sublime BRB (blueberry, ricotta and bacon) pancakes. (☏6298 2420; www.artistryspace.com; 17 Jln Pinang; ⏱10am-7pm Tue-Sun; 🛜; Ⓜ Bugis)

Maison Ikkoku
CAFE, COCKTAIL BAR

27 Map p96, E7

Pimped with Chesterfield banquettes and suspended dressers, Maison Ikkoku flies the flag for Third Wave Coffee, with brewing techniques such as Chemex, Syphon, Woodneck, French press, AeroPress and old-school espresso. Edibles include decent sandwiches, salads, cakes and *mi musubi*, a sushi-like Hawaiian snack topped with seasoned spam. Upstairs is the well-regarded cocktail bar, where crafty libations come with a view of Sultan Mosque's golden dome. (www.maison-ikkoku.net; 20 Kandahar St; ⏱cafe 9am-9pm Mon-Thu, to 11pm Fri & Sat, to 7pm Sun, bar 4pm-1am Sun-Thu, to 2am Fri & Sat; 🛜; Ⓜ Bugis)

Bar Stories
COCKTAIL BAR

28 Map p96, D7

Call ahead if heading here later in the week – this upstairs cocktail den is as small as it is hugely popular. If you're lucky, you'll be sitting at the bar, where gung-ho barkeeps keep it freestyle, turning whatever spirit or flavour turns you on into a smashing libation. Creative, whimsical and often brilliant. (☏6298 0838; www.barstories.

com.sg; 55/57A Haji Lane; ⏰3pm-1am Sun-Thu, to 2am Fri & Sat; Ⓜ Bugis)

Piedra Negra
BAR, RESTAURANT

29 Map p96, E8

With sexy Latin beats, bombastic murals and tables right on free-spirited Haji Lane, this electric Mexican joint is a brilliant spot for a little evening people-watching, any night of the week. Frozen or shaken, the margaritas pack a punch, and the joint's burritos, quesadillas, tacos and other Tex-Mex staples are filling and delish. (www.piedra-negra.com; cnr Beach Rd & Haji Lane; ⏰noon-midnight Mon-Thu, to 2am Fri, 5pm-2am Sat; Ⓜ Bugis)

Divine Bar
BAR

30 Map p96, D8

Looking straight out of 1930s Manhattan, this wine and cocktail lounge is an art deco–inspired extravaganza, adorned with ornate bronze ceilings, a grand piano and a 12m-high wine rack. Order a bottle after 6pm and the in-house wine angel 'flies up' to fetch your Shiraz (ignore the pulley). Of course, it just wouldn't be New York with live jazz, nightly from 8.15pm. (www.parkviewsquare.com; 600 North Bridge Rd, Parkview Square lobby; ⏰11am-12.30am; Ⓜ Bugis)

Bellwethers
BAR

31 Map p96, D4

Breezy Bellwethers brings a little hipster cool to the raffish streets of Little India. Grab an oil-drum table on the alleyway and neck a craft beer, whisky or just a decent cup of Joe. The grub is also good, whether it's snack-friendly *jamón*-wrapped grilled eggplant, or bigger, mostly meaty mains. Happy hour rocks on till 9pm. (www.bellwethers.com.sg; 120 Desker Rd; ⏰5-11.30pm Tue-Thu, 5pm-1am Fri, 11am-1am Sat, 11am-11pm Sun; 🛜; Ⓜ Farrer Park)

Prince of Wales
PUB

32 Map p96, B5

The closest thing to a pub in Little India, this grungy Aussie hang-out doubles as a backpacker hostel. It's an affable, popular spot, with a small beer garden, a pool table, sports screens and live music several times a week. Weekly staples include Wednesday Quiz Night (from 8pm) and the Sunday Session, complete with BBQ (3.30pm to 7.30pm) and music jams (from 4pm). (www.facebook.com/POW.Little.India; 101 Dunlop St; ⏰8.30am-1am Sun-Thu, to 2am Fri & Sat; Ⓜ Little India)

Ⓠ Local Life
Bollywood at the Rex

Where can you catch the Bollywood blockbusters advertised all over Little India? Why at the **Rex Cinemas** (Map p96, A5; http://tickets.rexcinema.com.sg; 2 Mackenzie Rd; tickets $15; Ⓜ Little India), of course. This historic theatre, on the very edge of the neighbourhood, screens films from around the subcontinent, most subtitled in English.

Entertainment

BluJaz Café

LIVE MUSIC

33 ⭐ Map p96, E7

Bohemian pub BluJaz is one of your best options for live music in town, with regular jazz jams and other acts playing anything from blues to rockabilly. Check the website for the list of rotating events, which include DJ-spun funk, R&B and retro nights, and Wednesday's 'Talk Cock' open-mic comedy night. (www.blujaz.net; 11 Bali Lane; entry from $6; ⏱noon-1am Mon-Thu, noon-2am Fri, 4pm-2am Sat; Ⓜ Bugis)

Bian's Cafe

CHINESE OPERA

34 ⭐ Map p96, E7

Visit this quaint cafe between 3pm and 6pm on Thursday afternoon and you'll be treated to short bursts of Beijing opera tunes. You may even be able to have a go yourself; Chinese opera karaoke, anyone? The site is also home to the grandly named **Singapore Chinese Opera Museum** (admission $5), which documents the history and development of the art form in Singapore. (www.singopera.com.sg; 100 Jln Sultan, 01-27, Sultan Plaza; admission $10; ⏱11am-7pm Mon-Fri; Ⓜ Bugis)

Wild Rice

THEATRE

35 ⭐ Map p96, A4

Singapore's sexiest theatre group is based in Kerbau Rd, but performs shows elsewhere in the city (as well as abroad). Productions range from farce to serious politics, and fearlessly wade into issues not commonly on the agenda in Singapore.(☑6292 2695; www.wildrice.com.sg; 65 Kerbau Rd; Ⓜ Little India)

Bugis+

MALL

36 ⭐ Map p96, C8

This futuristic, Gen-Y mall packs a virtual punch with its screen-centric thrills and spills Join gaming geeks at **St Games** (www.stgamescafe.com; 03-16/17, Bugis+; ⏱11.30am-9.30pm Sun-Thu, to midnight Fri & Sat) or the epic **Garena Stadium** (http://stadium.garena.com; 03-19, Bugis+), or get nostalgic at amusement parlour **Arcadia** (05-04/05, Bugis+; ⏱11am-11pm Sun-Thu, to 1am Fri & Sat). Alternatively, channel your inner Lorde in one of the themed karaoke lounges at **K Suites** (www.ksuites.com.sg; 03-18, Bugis+). Level 4 houses a plethora of funky, food-court-style eateries. (www.bugis-plus.com.sg; 201 Victoria St; Ⓜ Bugis).

Hood

LIVE MUSIC

Inside the Bugis+ mall (see 36 ⭐ Map p96, C8), Hood's street-art interior sets a youthful scene for nightly music jams with acts such as Rush Hour and Smells like Last Friday. If it's undiscovered talent you're after, head in for the weekly 'Saturday Original Sessions', a showcase for budding musos itching to share their singer-songwriter skills. (www.hoodbarandcafe.com; 201 Victoria St, 05-07, Bugis+; ⏱5pm-1am Mon & Tue, to 3am Wed-Fri, noon-3am Sat, noon-1am Sun; Ⓜ Bugis, City Hall)

Shopping

Sifr Aromatics

PERFUME

37 🔒 Map p96, E7

This Zen-like perfume laboratory belongs to third-generation perfumer Johari Kazura, whose exquisite creations include the heady East (50mL $140), a blend of oud, rose absolute, amber and neroli. Perfumes range from $85 to $300 for 50mL, while vintage perfume bottles range from $60 to $2000. Those after a custom-made fragrance should call a couple of days ahead before their visit. (www.sifr.sg; 42 Arab St; ⏰11am-8.30pm Mon-Sat, to 5pm Sun; Ⓜ Bugis)

Tuckshop & Sundry Supplies

FASHION, ACCESSORIES

38 🔒 Map p96, D7

A vintage-inspired ode to Americana working-class culture, this super-cool menswear store offers a clued-in selection of rugged threads and accessories, including designer eyewear, grooming products and made-in-house leathergoods. Stock up on plaid shirts, sweat tops and harder-to-find denim from brands like Japan's Iron Heart and China's Red Cloud. (25 Bali Lane; ⏰11am-9pm Mon-Sat, noon-6pm Sun; Ⓜ Bugis)

Little Shophouse

HANDICRAFTS

39 🔒 Map p96, E7

Traditional Peranakan beadwork is a dying art, but it's kept very much alive in this quaint shop-cum-workshop. Starting at around $300, the shop's colourful slippers are designed by craftsman Robert Sng and hand-beaded by his sister, Irene. While they're not cheap, each pair takes a painstaking two months to complete. Beadwork aside, you'll also find Peranakan-style tea sets, crockery, vases, handbags and jewellery. (43 Bussorah St; ⏰10am-5pm; Ⓜ Bugis)

🔍 Local Life
Jalan Besar

Once better known for its hardware stores and boxing matches, Jalan Besar is metamorphising into an area where heritage architecture meets new-school Singapore cool. It's a compact district, centred on Jalan Besar and Tyrwhitt Rd. It's on the latter that you'll find cult-status cafe-roaster **Chye Seng Huat Hardware** (Map p96,E2; www.cshhcoffee.com; 150 Tyrwhitt Rd; ⏰9am-7pm Tue-Fri, to 10pm Sat & Sun; Ⓜ Lavender). Right above it sits **Tyrwhitt General Company** (Map p96, E2; http://tyrwhittgeneralcompany.com; 150A Tyrwhitt Rd; ⏰11am-7pm Tue-Sun; Ⓜ Lavender), a shop-workshop peddling handmade jewellery, art and knickknacks, most of it designed and made in Singapore. To get here, alight at Lavendar MRT station and walk northwest up Horne Rd to Tyrwhitt Rd.

THEGENERALCO.SG ©

Craft workshop, Tyrwhitt General Company (p109)

Nalli

CLOTHING

40 🔒 Map p96, A5

For better quality cotton and silk saris, try this small industrious shop on Buffalo Rd. You can pick up cotton saris for as little as $30. The beautiful silk versions, most of which are upstairs, go for between $100 and $1000. (www.nallisingapore.com.sg; 10 Buffalo Rd; ⊘10am-9.30pm Mon-Sat, to 7.30pm Sun; Ⓜ Little India)

Bugis Street Market

MARKET

41 🔒 Map p96, C7

What was once Singapore's most infamous sleaze pit – packed with foreign servicemen on R&R, gambling dens and 'sisters' (transvestites) – is now its most famous undercover street market, crammed with cheap clothes, shoes, accessories, manicurists, food stalls and, in a nod to its past, a sex shop. (www.bugis-street.com; Victoria St; ⊘11am-10pm; Ⓜ Bugis)

Bugis Junction

MALL

42 🔒 Map p96, C8

Featuring two streets of glassed-in, air-conditioned shophouse re-creations, Bugis Junction lures teens and 20-somethings with its fast fashion, costume jewellery, *kawaii* collectables and street-smart backpacks and courier bags. Global brands include concept store **Muji** and a small branch of bookstore **Kinokuniya**. (200 Victoria St; ⏰10am-10pm; Ⓜ Bugis)

Mustafa Centre   DEPARTMENT STORE

43 🔒 Map p96, C3

Little India's bustling 24-hour Mustafa Centre is a magnet for budget shoppers, most of them from the subcontinent. It's a sprawling place, peddling everything from electronics and garish gold jewellery to shoes, bags, luggage and beauty products. There's also a large supermarket with a great range of Indian foodstuffs. If you can't handle crowds, avoid the place on Sunday. (www.mustafa.com.sg; 145 Syed Alwi Rd; ⏰24hr; Ⓜ Farrer Park)

Sim Lim Square   ELECTRONICS, MALL

44 🔒 Map p96, B6

A byword for all that is cut-price and geeky, Sim Lim is jammed with stalls selling motherboards, soundcards, games consoles, laptops and cameras. If you know what you're doing, there are some deals to be had, but the untutored are more likely to be taken for a ride. Hard bargaining is essential. (www.simlimsquare.com.sg; 1 Rochor Canal Rd; ⏰11am-8pm; Ⓜ Bugis)

Basheer Graphic Books   BOOKS

45 🔒 Map p96, B8

Spruce up your coffee table at this cornucopia of graphic books and magazines. Located inside the Bras Basah Complex (locally dubbed 'Book City'), you'll find everything from fashion and design tomes to titles on art, architecture and urban planning. The shop also does a brisk mail-order business, so if you're mid-travel and want to have something mailed to you, staff are happy to help. (www.facebook.com/BasheerGraphic; 231 Bain St, 04-19, Bras Basah Complex; ⏰10am-8pm Mon-Sat, 11am-6pm Sun; Ⓜ Bugis, City Hall)

Straits Records   MUSIC

46 🔒 Map p96, E7

Hiding up a set of stairs, Straits Records is one of the few alternative music stores in Singapore. Stock includes hip hop, hardcore and reggae CDs, as well as some old vinyl, T-shirts and books. CDs from local bands start at around $10. (24A Bali Lane; ⏰3-10pm Mon-Fri, 2-10pm Sat, 2-8pm Sun; Ⓜ Bugis)

🔍 Local Life

Haji Lane

Fashion fiends in search of lesser-known (and locally grown) labels flock to **Haji Lane** (Map p96, E7; Haji Lane; Ⓜ Bugis), a pastel-hued strip in Kampong Glam lined with hipster-approved, one-off boutiques. **Dulcetfig** (Map p96, E7; www.dulcetfig.com; 41 Haji Lane; ⏰noon-9pm Mon-Thu, to 10pm Fri & Sat, noon-8pm Sun; Ⓜ Bugis) drives female fashion bloggers wild with its cool local and foreign frocks and accessories, which include high-end vintage bags and jewellery.

Explore

Sentosa

Epitomised by its star attraction, Universal Studios, Sentosa is essentially one giant Pleasure Island. The choices are head-spinning, from duelling roller coasters and indoor skydiving to stunt shows and luge racing. Add to this a historic fort, state-of-the-art aquarium and Ibiza-inspired beachside bars and restaurants, and it's clear why locals head here to live a little.

The Sights in a Day

Only the truly insane would attempt to experience all of Sentosa's attractions in one day, so choose a few and enjoy them thoroughly. You could easily spend the entire day lapping up the rides, shows, food and shops at **Universal Studios** (p114).

Feast on Malay hawker favourites at **Malaysian Food Street** (p120), then spend the afternoon at Universal Studios. Explore the deep at **S.E.A. Aquarium** (p117), or dabble in history at **Images of Singapore** (p119) or **Fort Siloso** (p119). Adrenalin junkie options include indoor skydiving at **iFly** (p118) and luge racing at **Sentosa Luge & Skyride** (p118), while those who prefer their thrills dripping wet should head to **Wave House** (p118) or **Adventure Cove Waterpark** (p117).

Slide into evening with sunset mojitos at **Coastes** (p121), **Tanjong Beach Club** (p121) or **Woobar** (p121), then dine marina-side at **Mykonos on the Bay** (p120) or **Sabio by the Sea** (p120). For sheer romance and a fine-dining menu, book a table at discrete, hilltop **Cliff** (p120).

Top Sights
Universal Studios (p114)

Best of Singapore

Food & Drink
Cliff (p120)

Malaysian Food Street (p120)

Kith Cafe (p120)

Thrills & Spills
Universal Studios (p114)

iFly (p118)

Wave House (p118)

For Families
Universal Studios (p114)

Adventure Cove Waterpark (p117)

Songs of the Sea (p121)

Getting There

Cable car Ride the cable car from Mt Faber or the HarbourFront Centre.

Monorail The Sentosa Express (7am to midnight) connects VivoCity to three stations on Sentosa: Waterfront, Imbiah and Beach.

Walk Simply walk across the Sentosa Boardwalk from VivoCity.

Top Sights
Universal Studios

Hankering for a little unadulterated fun? Then Universal Studios is looking at you, kid. The top-draw attraction at Resorts World, its booty of rides, roller coasters, shows, shops and restaurants are neatly packaged into fantasy-world themes based on your favourite Hollywood films. Attractions span the toddler-friendly to the seriously gut-wrenching, spread across a storybook landscape of castles, temples, jungles, retro Americana and sci-fi fantasy. Big kid or small, expect to leave with a blockbuster grin.

👁 Map p116; D2

www.rwsentosa.com

Resorts World

adult/child/senior $74/54/36

🕐 10am-7pm daily

🚌 Waterfront

Don't Miss

Battlestar Galactica

If you're a hard-core thrill-seeker, strap yourself onto Battlestar Galactica, the world's tallest duelling roller coasters. Choose between the sit-down Human roller coaster or the Cylon, an inverted roller coaster with multiple loops and flips. If you can pull your attention away from screaming, be sure to enjoy the bird's-eye view, not to mention the refreshing breeze.

Transformers The Ride

This exhilarating, next-generation motion thrill ride deploys high-definition 3D animation to transport you to a dark, urban otherworld where you'll be battling giant menacing robots, engaging in high-speed chases and even plunging off the edge of a soaring skyscraper. It's an incredibly realistic, adrenalin-pumping experience that will leave you lining up for a second fix.

Revenge of the Mummy

The main attraction of the park's Ancient Egypt section, Revenge of the Mummy will have you twisting, dipping and hopping in darkness on your search for the Book of the Living. Contrary to Hollywood convention, your journey ends with a surprising, fiery twist.

WaterWorld

Gripping stunts, fiery explosions and ridiculously fit eye candy is what you get at WaterWorld, a spectacular live show based on the Kevin Costner flick. Head here at least 20 minutes before show time if you want a decent seat. For a drenching, sit in the soak zone right at the front.

UNIVERSAL STUDIOS SINGAPORE, RESORTS WORLD SENTOSA ©

☑ Top Tips

▶ Skip entry queues by buying tickets online.

▶ Friday to Sunday is busiest, Wednesday morning is generally quietest. Avoid public holidays altogether.

▶ Consider wearing flip-flops (thongs), especially if you plan on hitting water-themed rides like Rapids Adventure.

▶ The lockers just to the right of the entrance to Universal Studios are cheaper than those inside the theme park. Pass-outs are allowed.

✕ Take a Break

Cafes and restaurants throughout Universal Studios serve Western and Asian dishes.

For authentic Malaysian hawker food, opt for Malaysian Food Street (p120), an indoor hawker centre just outside the theme-park entrance.

E

Pulau
Brani

Street 8

Brani Terminal Ave

Selat
Sengkir

Serapong Golf
Course

Allanbrooke Rd

17 ◉🅱◎✕

12

13 ✕◎ ✕◎ 14

Bukit Manis Rd

Tanjong
Golf
Course

11 ◎✕

15 🅱✕

Tanjong
Beach

D

Sentosa Gateway

Causeway
Bridge

Gateway Ave

◉ S.E.A.
Aquarium

Sentosa Gateway Bridge

1 ◎

Resorts
World

◉ Universal
Studios

The Knolls

Artillery Ave

C

Kappel
Harbour

Adventure Cove
Waterpark

2 ◎

Butterfly Park &
Insect Kingdom

Waterfront ◉
Merlion 🅱
Plaza

Sentosa
Cable Car
Station 🅱

9 ◎

8 ◎

Imbiah 🅱
Beach
View

3 ◎

iFly

Cable Car Rd

Images of
Singapore

Beach 🅱

18 ✪

◎ Cogreen Segway
10 ◎ Eco Adventure

Palawan
Beach

B

Mt Imbiah ▲

Imbiah Walk

Siloso Rd

5 ◎

Sentosa Luge
& Skyride

16 🅱

4 ◎

Wave
House

6 ◎

MegaZip

Siloso
Beach

Sebarok Channel

A

7 ◎ Fort
Siloso

◉ N

0 ──── 500 m
0 ──── 0.25 miles

1 2 3 4

SHIRLYN LOO/GETTY IMAGES ©

S.E.A Aquarium

Sights

S.E.A. Aquarium
AQUARIUM

1  Map p116, D1

You'll be gawking at over 800 species of aquatic creatures at the world's biggest aquarium. It's a sprawling, state-of-the-art complex that re-creates 49 aquatic habitats found between Southeast Asia, Australia and Africa. The Open Ocean habitat is especially spectacular; its viewing panel (36m long, 8.3m high) is the world's largest. Adjoining the aquarium is the interactive **Maritime Experiential Museum**, which explores the history of the maritime Silk Route. (www.rwsentosa.com; Resorts World; adult/child incl entry to Maritime Experiential Museum $38/28; ☉10am-7pm)

Adventure Cove Waterpark
SWIMMING

2  Map p116, C1

The choice of rides at this water park is somewhat limited and better suited to kids and families. That said, adult thrill-seekers will appreciate the Riptide Rocket (a hydro-magnetic coaster), Pipeline Plunge and Bluewater Bay, a wave pool with serious gusto. Rainbow Reef sees you snorkelling among 20,000 fish, and for an extra charge, you can wade with stingrays. The popular Dolphin Island attraction allows visitors to interact with

Local Life
Endless Summer Pool Party

The jaw-dropping pool of the **W Singapore - Sentosa Cove hotel** (see 17 Map p116, E3; www.wsingaporesentosacove.com) is the setting for its hugely popular pool party **Endless Summer**. Usually held on the first Sunday of the month, it draws a diverse crowd of locals, expats and hotel guests, both straight and gay, young and not so young. It's a fabulous way to spend a lazy, boozy, tropical afternoon, with DJ sets, live music, and no shortage of oversized sunglasses, bikinis and six-packs. Visit the hotel website for dates and to book.

dolphins, though it has received criticism from animal welfare groups. (www.rwsentosa.com; Resorts World Sentosa; adult/child $36/26; 10am-6pm)

iFly
INDOOR SKYDIVING

3 Map p116, C2

If you fancy freefalling from 12,000ft to 3,000ft *without* leaping out of a plane, leap into this indoor skydiving centre. The price includes an hour's instruction followed by two short but thrilling skydives in a vertical wind chamber. Check the website for off-peak times, which offer the cheapest rates. (www.iflysingapore.com; Cable Car Rd; adult/child from $79/70; 10.30am-10pm Thu-Tue, noon-10pm Wed)

Wave House
SURFING

4 Map p116, B2

Two specially designed wave pools allow surf dudes and dudettes to practise their gashes and their cutbacks at ever-popular Wave House. The non-curling Double Flowrider is good for beginners, while the 10ft FlowBarrel is more challenging. Wave House also includes beachside eating and drinking options. (www.wavehousesentosa.com; Siloso Beach; 30min surf sessions from $35/60; 10.30am-10.30pm, Double Flowrider 11am-10pm, FlowBarrel 1-10pm Mon, Tue, Thu & Fri, 11am-10pm Wed, Sat & Sun)

Sentosa Luge & Skyride
THRILL RIDE

5 Map p116, C2

Take the skyride chairlift from Siloso Beach to Imbiah Lookout, then hop onto your luge and race family and friends through hairpin bends and bone-shaking straights carved through the forest – helmets are provided and mandatory! (1/2/3/5 rides $12.50/18/22/30; 10am-9.30pm)

MegaZip
ZIPLINING

6 Map p116, B2

Check out this 450m-long, 75m-tall zipline from Imbiah Lookout to a tiny island off Siloso Beach. An electric cart is on hand to shuttle riders up from the beach to the start point, where there's also a small adventure park with a climbing wall ($19) and other activities. (www.megazip.com.sg; Siloso Beach; zipline ride $39; 11am-7pm)

Fort Siloso
MUSEUM

7 ◉ Map p116, A1

Dating from the 1880s, when Sentosa was called Pulau Blakang Mati (Malay for 'the island behind which lies death'), this British coastal fort proved famously useless during the Japanese invasion of 1942. Documentaries, artefacts, animatronics and re-created historical scenes talk visitors through the fort's history, and the underground tunnels are fun to explore. (www.sentosa.com.sg; Siloso Point; adult/child $12/9; ◷10am-6pm, free guided tours 12.40pm & 3.40pm Fri-Sun)

Images of Singapore
MUSEUM

8 ◉ Map p116, C2

This interactive museum uses wax dummies, film footage and dramatic light-and-sound effects to traverse seven centuries of Singapore history. Kicking off with Singapore's Malay sultanate days, exhibits weave their way through its consolidation as a port and trading centre, WWII and the subsequent Japanese surrender. (www.sentosa.com.sg; Imbiah Lookout; adult/child $10/7; ◷9am-7pm)

Butterfly Park & Insect Kingdom
WILDLIFE RESERVE

9 ◉ Map p116, B1

A tropical rainforest in miniature, the Butterfly Park claims over 50 species of butterflies, many of which are endangered and nearly all of which have been bred in the park itself. Critters at the Insect Kingdom include thousands of mounted butterflies, rhino beetles, Hercules beetles (the world's largest) and scorpions. (www.sentosa.com.sg; 51 Imbiah Rd, Imbiah Lookout; adult/child $16/10; ◷9.30am-7pm; monorail Imbiah)

Gogreen Segway Eco Adventure
TOUR

10 ◉ Map p116, C2

These two-wheeled transporters will have you zipping around a 10-minute 'fun ride' circuit or, if you prefer, exploring the beachfront on a guided Eco Adventure trip. Equally futuristic are the electric bikes, yours to hire for $12 an hour. Eco Adventure riders must be at least 10 years old. (☎9825 4066; www.segway-sentosa.com; fun rides $12, 30min eco adventures $38; ◷10am-8pm)

☑ Top Tip

Entrance Fee & Transport

The entrance fee to Sentosa varies according to the transport chosen: pedestrians walking from VivoCity pay $1, passengers on the Sentosa Express monorail pay $4, while cable-car passengers have the entrance fee included in the price of the ticket. Once on the island, it's easy to get around, either by walking, taking the Sentosa Express (7am to midnight), riding the free 'beach tram' (shuttling the length of all three beaches) or by using the three free colour-coded bus routes that link the main attractions. On Sentosa, the monorail, tram and buses are free.

Eating

Cliff
INTERNATIONAL $$$

11 ✕ Map p116, E4

Perched high above Palawan Beach (although tree cover obscures some of the view), fine-dining Cliff is set by the dreamy swimming-pool area of luxury hotel Sentosa Resort. Book two weeks ahead to secure a coveted table by the balcony's edge – an especially evocative spot to savour artful dishes with predominantly French and Italian influences. Vegetarian options are few and far between. (✆6371 1425; www.sentosadining.com.sg; 2 Bukit Manis Rd, Sentosa Resort; mains $28-98; ⏲6.30-10pm)

Mykonos on the Bay
GREEK $$

12 ✕ Map p116, E3

At Sentosa Cove, this slick, marina-flanking taverna serves up Hellenic flavours that could make your *papou* weep. Sit alfresco and tuck into perfectly charred, marinated octopus, aubergine salad and housemade *giaourtlou* (spicy lamb sausage). Book ahead later in the week. (✆6334 3818; www.mykonosonthebay.com; 01-10 Quayside Isle, 31 Ocean Way, Sentosa Cove; tapas $9-27, mains $23-45; ⏲6.30-10.30pm Mon-Wed, noon-2.30pm & 6.30-10.30pm Thu & Fri, noon-10.30pm Sat & Sun; ✎)

Sabio by the Sea
SPANISH $$

13 ✕ Map p116, E3

One of a row of waterside restaurants at Sentosa Cove, stylish Sabio is a gorgeous spot for languid tropical evenings drinking Caipirinhas, grazing on tapas and fantasing about the millionaire boats moored before you. Winning tapas include the garlicky mushrooms, fluffy croquetas stuffed with gooey Manchego cheese and the beautifully grilled vegetables. Figure three plates per person. (✆6690 7568; sabio.sg/bythesea; 31 Ocean Way, 01-02; tapas $6-22, paella from $25; ⏲noon-10pm Mon-Thu, noon-10.30pm Fri & Sat, 10.30am-10pm Sun; ✿)

Malaysian Food Street
HAWKER CENTRE $

With its faux Malaysian streetscape, this indoor hawker centre beside Universal Studios (see ◉ Map p116, D2), feels a bit Disney. Thankfully, there's nothing fake about the food, cooked by some of Malaysia's best hawker vendors. (www.rwsentosa.com; Resorts World; snacks from $1, dishes from $3; ⏲11am-10pm Mon-Thu, 9am-11pm Fri & Sat, 9am-10pm Sun)

Kith Cafe
CAFE $$

14 ✕ Map p116, E3

This is the best of Kith's trio of outlets, set beside million-dollar yachts at salubrious Sentosa Cove. Grab a copy of Kinfolk, scan the crowd and tuck into fantastic cafe grub like Blackstone Eggs (English muffins with poached eggs, roasted tomatoes, bacon, grilled asparagus and hollandaise sauce). (www.kith.com.sg; 31 Ocean Way, Sentosa Cove; ⏲8am-10pm Wed-Mon; ✎)

Drinking

Tanjong Beach Club
BAR

15 Map p116, E4

Generally quieter than the bars on Siloso beach (except during the busy Sunday brunch session), Tanjong Beach Club is an evocative spot, with evening torches on the sand, a small stylish pool for guests and a sultry lounge-and-funk soundtrack. (☑6270 1355; www.tanjong-beachclub.com; Tanjong Beach; ⏰11am-11pm Tue-Fri, 10am-midnight Sat & Sun)

Coastes
BAR

16 Map p116, B2

More family-friendly than many of the other beach venues, Coastes has picnic tables on the sand and sun lounges ($20) by the water. If you're peckish, there's a comprehensive menu of decent standard offerings, including burgers, pasta and salads. (Siloso Beach; ⏰9am-11pm Sun-Thu, to 1am Fri & Sat)

Woobar
BAR

17 Map p116, E3

The W Singapore's hotel bar is glam and camp, with suspended egg-shaped pods, gold footrests and floor-to-ceiling windows looking out at palms and pool. The afternoon 'high tea' (from $58 for two, excluding tax) is served in dainty birdcages, while the weekly Wednesday Ladies' Night ($36 before tax) comes with free-pour champagne between 7.30pm and 9pm, followed by half-price drinks until midnight. (www.

PETER UNGER/GETTY IMAGES ©

Siloso Beach

wsingaporesentosacove.com; 21 Ocean Way, W Singapore, Sentosa Cove; ⏰8am-midnight Mon-Thu, to 2am Fri-Sun)

Entertainment

Songs of the Sea
THEATER

18 Map p116, C3

Set around a replica Malay fishing village, this ambitious show fuses Lloyd Webber–esque theatricality with an awe-inspiring sound, light and laser extravaganza worth a hefty $4 million. Prepare to gasp, swoon and (occasionally) cringe. (www.sentosa.com.sg; Siloso Beach; standard/premium seats $15/18; ⏰shows at 7.40pm & 8.40pm)

Top Sights
Singapore Zoo

Getting There

Singapore Zoo is 22km northwest of the CBD.

M MRT Catch the North-South (red) line to Ang Mo Kio, then bus 138 to the zoo.

While some of the world's zoos are boring or even cruel, Singapore Zoo is a verdant, tropical wonderland of spacious, naturalistic enclosures, freely roaming animals and interactive attractions. Breakfast with orang-utans, dodge flying foxes, mosey up to tree-hugging sloths, even snoop around a replica African village. Then there's the setting: 28 soothing hectares on a lush peninsula jutting out onto the waters of the Upper Seletar Reservoir. Miss it at your own peril.

Orang-utans

Don't Miss

Jungle Breakfast with Wildlife

Orang-utans are the zoo's celebrity residents and you can devour a scrumptious breakfast buffet in their company at **Jungle Breakfast with Wildlife** (adult/child $33/23; ⏱9-10.30am). If you miss out, get your photo taken with them at the neighbouring Free Ranging Orang-utan Island (11am and 3.30pm). Best of all, you're free to use your own camera.

Fragile Forest

Further close encounters await at the Fragile Forest, a giant bio-dome that replicates the stratas of a rainforest. Cross paths with free-roaming butterflies and colourful lories, swooping Malayan flying foxes and unperturbed ring-tailed lemurs. The pathway leads up to the forest canopy and the dome's most chilled-out locals, the two-toed sloths.

Great Rift Valley of Ethiopia

Featuring cliffs, a waterfall and a stream fashioned to look like the Ethiopian hinterland, the evocative Great Rift Valley exhibit is home to Hamadryas baboons, Nubian ibexes, banded mongooses, black-backed jackals and rock hyraxes. You'll also find replica Ethiopian villages, complete with dwelling huts and insight into the area's harsh living conditions.

Rainforest Kidzworld

Let your own little critters go wild at **Rainforest Kidzworld** (⏱8.30am-6pm), a technicolor play area complete with slides, swings, pulling boats and a carousel. Kids can also ride ponies, feed farmyard animals and squeal to their heart's content in the wet-play area. Swimwear is available for purchase on-site if you don't have your own.

☎6269 3411

www.zoo.com.sg

80 Mandai Lake Rd

adult/child $28/18

⏱8.30am-6pm

☑ Top Tips

▶ Consider combining your trip with a visit to the neighbouring Night Safari (p125).

▶ Wear comfortable shoes, a sunhat and sunglasses. Ponchos are available ($5) in case of rain. If you have kids, bring swimwear for Rainforest Kidzworld.

▶ Feeding times are staggered. Check the website for details.

✗ Take a Break

There's no shortage of eateries on-site, serving everything from thin-crust pizza and American fast food to local staples like laksa, Hainanese chicken rice and nasi lemak (rice boiled in coconut milk with fried ikan bilis, peanuts and a curry dish).

Top Sights
Night Safari

Getting There

Located beside the Singapore Zoo, Night Safari is 22km north-west of the CBD.

M **MRT** Catch the North-South (red) line to Ang Mo Kio, then bus 138 to the zoo.

Next door to Singapore Zoo, but completely separate, Singapore's acclaimed Night Safari offers a very different type of nightlife. Home to over 120 species of animals, the park's moats and barriers seem to melt away in the darkness, giving you the feeling of travelling through a thrilling jungle filled with the likes of lions, leopards and alligators. The atmosphere is heightened even further by the herds of strolling antelopes, often passing within inches of the trams that take you around.

Malayan tiger

Don't Miss

Electric Tram Tour
Almost everyone heads to the tram queue as they enter, and you should too. These near-silent, open-sided vehicles come with a guide whose commentary is a good introduction to the park's animals and different habitats. The journey lasts for 45 minutes, though we highly recommend that you alight at the designated stops to explore more of the park on foot. If possible, opt for the second or third cars as they offer the best view.

Walking Trails
The grounds offer four interlinked walking trails, each taking between 20 and 30 minutes to explore. Get centimetres away from wild spotted felines on the Leopard Trail, also home to the thrilling Giant Flying Squirrel aviary. Peer at splash-happy cats and the world's largest bat, the Malay flying fox, on the Fishing Cat Trail. The Wallaby Trail is home to a walk-through wallaby habitat, while the outstanding East Lodge Trail awaits with highly endangered babirusas and elegant Malay tigers.

Creatures of the Night
If you have kids in tow, don't miss **Creatures of the Night** (⏲shows 7.30pm, 8.30pm & 9.30pm, plus 10.30pm Fri & Sat), an interactive 20-minute show with stars that include binturongs, civets and an owl. Seating is unassigned, so it's a good idea to arrive a little early to secure a good vantage point. Note that shows may be cancelled in case of wet weather.

www.nightsafari.c

80 Mandai Lake Rd

adult/child $39/25

⏲7.30pm–midnight, restaurants & shops from 5.30pm

☑ Top Tips

▶ When returning from the safari, you should catch a bus at around 10.35pm as the last MRT train leaves Ang Mo Kio at 11.35pm. Otherwise, expect to pay around $23 for a taxi to the city centre.

▶ Wear comfortable shoes and bring insect repellent and an umbrella, just in case.

✕ Take a Break

Food and drink options abound outside the entrance. **Bongo Burgers** (⏲5.30pm–midnight) serves tasty burgers. For local specialities there's kampong-inspired **Ulu Ulu** (⏲5.30–11pm), with both à la carte options and a buffet.

Explore

Holland Village & Dempsey Hill

Chic, salubrious Holland Village may not be a must for visitors, but its boutiques, cafes and lunching ladies offer a revealing slice of expat life. Even leafier is historic Dempsey Hill, a converted barracks laced with antiques dealers, boutiques, cafes and languid bistros. Upstaging them both is the Botanic Gardens, an invigorating blend of rare orchids, precious rainforest and romantic dining.

The Sights in a Day

☀ Beat the heat with an early-morning saunter through the **Botanic Gardens** (p128), keeping cool in the ancient rainforest, circling Swan Lake and dropping in on Vanda Miss Joaquim, Singapore's national flower, at the National Orchid Centre. Appetite piqued, head across to **Chopsuey** (p132) for dim sum or **PS Cafe** (p132) for beautiful global fare, then shop-hop Dempsey Hill for antiques, art and accessories at stores like **Shang Antique** (p137) and **Em Gallery** (p137).

☀ Spend the afternoon in trendy, expat enclave Holland Village. Cool down with gourmet ice cream at **Daily Scoop** (p136) or a glass of vino at **Park** (p136). Refreshed, scour **Holland Village Shopping Centre** (p137) for arts, craft and knick-knacks, or head upstairs for a manicure.

☾ Come evening, head back to the Botanic Gardens for romantic noshing at **Halia** (p133) or heady, Ubud-style **Blue Bali** (p133). Alternatively, head back to Dempsey Hill for superlative seafood at **Long Beach Seafood** (p132), followed by craft suds at neighbouring **RedDot Brewhouse** (p136).

👁 Top Sights

Singapore Botanic Gardens (p128)

💗 Best of Singapore

Eating

Chopsuey (p132)

Halia (p133)

PS Cafe (p132)

Drinking

Red Dot Brewhouse (p136)

Shopping

Shang Antique (p137)

Getting There

Ⓜ **MRT** Holland Village and the Botanic Gardens both have their own MRT stops on the Yellow Line.

🚌 **Bus** To reach Dempsey Hill, catch bus 7, 75, 77, 105, 106, 123 or 174 from behind Orchard MRT, on Orchard Blvd. Buses 75 and 106 are two of several linking Dempsey Hill with Holland Village.

Top Sights
Singapore Botanic Gardens

For instant stress relief, take a dose of the Singapore Botanic Gardens. Suddenly the roar of traffic and 5.4 million voices melts into the branches, and the world is a tranquil, verdant paradise. At the tail end of Orchard Rd, Singapore's most famous sprawl of greenery offers more than just picnic-friendly lawns and lakes. It's home to ancient rainforest, themed gardens, rare orchids, free concerts and one of Singapore's most romantic nosh spots. Breathe in, breathe out.

◉ Map p130; G2

☏ 6471 7361

www.sbg.org.sg

1 Cluny Rd

garden admission free

◷ hours vary

🚌 7, 105, 123, 174, Ⓜ Botanic Gardens

Don't Miss

National Orchid Garden

The Botanic Gardens' now famous orchid breeding began in 1928 and you can get the historical low-down at the **National Orchid Garden** (1 Cluny Park Rd, Botanic Gardens; adult/child $5/free; ⏲8.30am-7pm). To date, its 3 hectares are home to over 1000 species and 2000 hybrids, around 600 of which are on display – the largest showcase of tropical orchids on Earth.

Rainforest

Older than the Botanic Gardens themselves, this precious patch of dense primeval rainforest offers a sample of the kind that once carpeted much of Singapore. Hit the rainforest boardwalk and surround yourself with 314 species of vegetation; over half are now considered rare in Singapore.

Ginger Garden

If you thought there was only one type of ginger, the compact Ginger Garden will set you straight. Located next to the National Orchid Garden, this 1-hectare space contains over 250 members of the Zingiberaceae family. It's also where you'll find ginger-centric restaurant Halia. A supporting cast of plants include the little-known Lowiaceae, with their orchid-like flowers.

Swan Lake

For lazy serenity and a touch of romanticism, it's hard to beat Swan Lake. One of three lakes in the Botanic Gardens, it's studded by a tiny island cluttered with nibong palms. Look out for the mute swans, imported all the way from Amsterdam.

☑ Top Tips

▶ Excellent, volunteer-run guided tours of the Botanic Gardens take place every Saturday. See the website for times and themes.

▶ Check the website for free opera concerts, occasionally held at the Botanic Gardens' Symphony Lake.

▶ Buy water when you see it, not when you need it: signage in the Botanic Gardens is not always consistent and backtracking is hardly fun, especially when you're thirsty.

✕ Take a Break

For a romantic nosh among the Botanic Garden's ginger plants, grab a table at Halia (p133).

Even more atmospheric is Indonesian restaurant Blue Bali (p133). Skirting the Botanical Gardens, its alfresco pavilions and cabanas look straight out of Ubud.

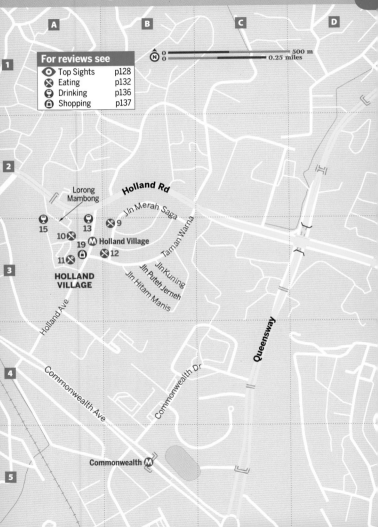

For reviews see

◉	Top Sights	p128
✕	Eating	p132
⊖	Drinking	p136
🔒	Shopping	p137

N 0 _____ 500 m
0 _____ 0.25 miles

A B C D

1 2 3 4 5

Lorong Mambong

Holland Rd

Jln Merah Saga

Taman Warna

Jln Kuning

Jln Puteh Jerneh

Jln Hitam Manis

15

13

9

10

19 Ⓜ Holland Village

11

12

HOLLAND VILLAGE

Holland Ave

Commonwealth Ave

Commonwealth Dr

Queensway

Commonwealth Ⓜ

E
Farrer Rd
M Farrer Rd

F

G
Cluny Park Rd
5 ✕

H
Evans Rd

1
8 ✕

Gallop Rd
Tyersall Rd
Symphony Lake
Singapore Botanic Gardens
◎
Cluny Rd
Nassim Rd

2
✕ 7
Singapore Botanic Gardens
Dalvey Gate Rd
Lermit Rd

Tyersall Ave
✕ 6
Cluny Rd

3

Swan Lake

DEMPSEY HILL
Dempsey Rd
Holland Rd
Napier Rd
Tanglin Golf Course

4
16 🔒
14
✕ 3
Dempsey Rd
18 🔒
Minden Rd
17 🔒 ✕ 2
✕ 4
Harding Rd
✕ 1
Loewen Rd
Tanglin Rd

5

Eating

Chopsuey   CHINESE $$

1 ✗ Map p130, F5

Swirling ceiling fans, crackly 1930s tunes and preened ladies on rattan chairs – Chopsuey has colonial chic down pat. It peddles revamped versions of retro American-Chinese dishes, but the real highlight here is the lunchtime yum cha. Standouts include Sichuan tofu, prawn dumplings and *san choi bao*. The marble bar is perfect for solo diners. (☏9224 6611; www.chopsueycafe.com; Block 10, Dempsey Rd; dim sum $7-15; ◷11.30am-4pm & 6.30-10.30pm Mon-Fri, 9.30am-4pm & 6.30-10.30pm Sat & Sun, bar to 11pm Sun-Thu, to 1am Fri & Sat; 🚍7, 75, 77, 105, 106, 123, 174)

◯ Local Life

Singapore Turf Club

Although not quite as manic as the Hong Kong races, a trip to **Singapore Turf Club** (www.turfclub.com.sg; 1 Turf Club Ave; Level 1 Grandstand & Level 2 Gallop $6, Owners' Lounge $30; Ⓜ Kranji) is nevertheless a hugely popular day out (bring your passport). Races usually run on Fridays (6.20pm to 10.50pm) and Sundays (12.50pm to 6.30pm) and a dress code is enforced: no jogging shorts or singlets in the public grandstand; no shorts, collarless T-shirts or sandals in the Owners' Lounge.

PS Cafe   INTERNATIONAL $$

2 ✗ Map p130, F4

A chic, light-filled tropical oasis of wooden floorboards, floor-to-ceiling windows and patio tables facing thick tropical foliage. From brunch to dinner, edibles are beautiful and healthy, whether it's fish croquette Benedict or a 'Morocco miracle stack' of roasted portobello mushroom, grilled vegetables, smoked eggplant and couscous. The weekend brunch is a no-bookings affair, so head in by 10.30am to avoid the longest queues. (☏9070 8782; www.pscafe.com; 28B Harding Rd; mains $23-36; ◷11.30am-3.30pm & 6.30-10.30pm; ✉; 🚍7, 75, 77, 105, 106, 123, 174)

Long Beach Seafood   SEAFOOD $$$

3 ✗ Map p130, F4

One of Singapore's top seafood restaurant chains. Settle in on the verandah, gaze out at thick forest and tackle the cult-status black-pepper crab. The original Long Beach lays claim to inventing the iconic dish, and the version here is fantastically peppery and earthy. (☏6323 2222; www.longbeachseafood.com.sg; 25 Dempsey Rd, 01-01; crab per kg around $60; ◷11am-3pm & 5.30pm-1.30am; 🚍7, 75, 77, 105, 106, 123, 174)

White Rabbit   INTERNATIONAL $$$

4 ✗ Map p130, G4

Dempsey Hill's garrison church has been reborn as a sophisticated, white-washed dining room and bar. Find the light in tweaked Euro comforters like tagliatelle pasta with Alaskan king crab, pork broth and kombu; 36-hour short ribs with truffle miso glaze; or warm banana pudding with ginger anglaise. Weekend brunch (10.30am to 3pm) combines standard menu items with breakfast staples like eggs and French toast. (www.thewhiterabbit.com.sg; 39C Harding Rd; 2/3 course set lunch menus from $32/38, mains $32-52; ☺noon-2.30pm & 6.30-10.30pm Tue-Fri, 10.30am-3pm & 6.30-10.30pm Sat & Sun; ☐7, 75, 77, 105, 106, 123, 174)

Holland Village Market & Food Centre (p134)

Blue Bali   INDONESIAN $$

5 🍴 Map p130, G1

Skirting the Botanic Gardens, Blue Bali is an enchanting dreamscape of Balinese wooden pavilions, cabanas over water and sarong-wrapped staff. Head in for a romantic sundowner and tapas-style bites such as Javanese satay, fried homemade tofu or chilli-spiked pumpkin prawns, all of which better suit the low tables than the mains. Great happy hour deals run from 5pm to 8pm. (☑6733 0185; www.bluebali.sg; 1D Cluny Rd; tapas $8-20, mains $16-32; ☺3pm-midnight Tue-Sun; 🛜; Ⓜ Botanic Gardens)

Halia   FUSION $$$

6 🍴 Map p130, G3

Atmospheric Halia is surrounded by the Botanic Gardens' ginger plants, a fact echoed in a number of unusual ginger-based dishes. Menus are a competent, fusion affair (think chilli crab spaghettini or Parmesan and almond-crusted stingray), and the weekday set lunch (two/three courses $28/32) is especially

good value. There's a dedicated vegetarian dinner menu, and at weekends you can also come for brunch (10am to 4pm) or English tea (3 to 5pm). (☑6476 6711; www.halia.com.sg; 1 Cluny Rd, Singapore Botanic Gardens; mains $28-68, dinner set menu $88-98, English tea $28; ☺noon-4pm & 6-10pm Mon-Fri, 10am-5pm & 6-10pm Sat & Sun; 🍴; Ⓜ Botanic Gardens)

Casa Verde   INTERNATIONAL $$

7 🍴 Map p130, G2

The most accessible and family-friendly restaurant in the Botanic Gardens, 'Green House' serves up decent Western grub (pasta, salads, sandwiches) plus wood-fired pizzas and a smattering of local dishes. (1 Cluny Rd, Singapore Botanic Gardens; lunches

$9-18, pizzas $21-25, dinner mains $25-30; ⏲7.30am-9.30pm; 🚻; Ⓜ Botanic Gardens)

Food Canopy
HAWKER CENTRE $

8 🍽 Map p130, H1

You'll find this breezy collection of hawker stalls outside the Botanic Gardens' Healing Garden. There's no shortage of favourites, from *kaya* toast and *kopi* (coffee) to roasted duck, ginseng chicken soup, Korean *bibimbap* and Indian *rojak*. The Tom Yam Fried Fish Bee Hoon from the Handmade Noodles stall is especially good. If coming by taxi, tell the driver it's next to the Raffles Building. (1J Cluny Rd; dishes from $3; ⏲7am-8pm; Ⓜ Botanic Gardens)

Da Paolo Pizza Bar
ITALIAN $$

9 🍽 Map p130, B3

The successful Da Paolo chain has two outlets on this street alone: a deli-cafe (at No 43) and this polished bistro

Local Life

Temple Yoga

If the sound of yoga in a Hindu temple makes your chakras glow, **Sri Muneeswaran Hindu Temple** (Commonwealth Drive; Ⓜ Commonwealth) should be on your hit list. Believed to be the largest shrine for the deity Sri Muneeswaran in Southeast Asia, it offers free hatha yoga classes on Sundays and Mondays (6pm to 7pm and 7pm to 8pm), with a dedicated class for children on Sundays (5.30pm to 7pm).

with terrace seating. Under a cowhide ceiling, svelte expats nosh on delicious thin-crust pizzas, competent pastas and a showstopping warm peanut butter caramel chocolate brownie. There's a good-value set lunch ($23) and a two-for-one happy hour from noon to 2.30pm and 5.30pm to 7.30pm. (www. dapaolo.com.sg; 44 Jln Merah Saga; pizzas $19-29, pasta $22-28; ⏲noon-2.30pm & 5.30-10.30pm Mon-Fri, 11am-10.30pm Sat & Sun; Ⓜ Holland Village)

Holland Village Market & Food Centre
HAWKER CENTRE $

10 🍽 Map p130, A3

Avoid the run-of-the-mill restaurants across the street and join the locals for cheap, scrumptious Singapore grub. A small clutch of stalls sell chicken rice, prawn noodles and other hawker staples. If you're new to the hawker food scene, there's a handy signboard outside that gives the low-down on the most popular dishes. (Lor Mambong; dishes from $3; ⏲10am-late; Ⓜ Holland Village)

2am Dessert Bar
DESSERT $$

11 🍽 Map p130, A3

Posh desserts with wine and cocktail pairings is the deal at this swanky hideout. While the menu includes savoury grub like burgers and beef-cheek croquettes, you're here for Janice Wong's sweet showstoppers, from basil white chocolate to purple potato puree with blackberry parfait, lavender marshmallows and fruits of the forest sorbet. Book ahead if heading here Thursday to Saturday

Understand

A Political Primer

Politics in Singapore is both everywhere and nowhere.

Everywhere, in the sense that everything you see, read and hear – with the increasingly significant exception of the web pages that pop up on the computer screens of Singapore's citizens – has at some point felt the guiding hand of government. But it's nowhere, in that the ebb and flow of conflicting opinions and ideas in a public forum is almost nonexistent.

Sole Political Force

The People's Action Party (PAP) has held power in Singapore since 1959 and has been virtually the sole political force since 1965, when the island was evicted from the Malay Federation after an uneasy alliance forged in 1963. Prime Minister Lee Kuan Yew famously cried on TV the day Singapore was left to fend for itself, but he's shed few tears since.

The white-clad party he led with steely paternalism is still in control and is currently led by his son, Lee Hsien Loong. Opposition voices have been removed from the political process via lawsuits and financial ruin. (According to Singapore law, bankrupted citizens aren't allowed to run for election.) Many Singaporeans find persuasive the argument that a successful government doesn't need challenging, while others believe that the government – precisely because of its success – ought to be more tolerant of criticism.

Appetite for Change

In 2006 the ruling PAP won the expected majority in a landslide victory, claiming 82 of the 84 seats in parliament, but their actual votes fell by 8.69%. The appetite for change was even clearer with the election of 2011, which had the highest proportion of contested seats (94.3%) since Singapore's independence in 1965. The PAP lost a further 6.46% of the electorate, gaining 60.14% of the votes and 81 of the 87 seats. The biggest gains went to the Worker's Party (WP), whose political agenda puts the spotlight on concerns facing the average Singaporean. Among these is the rising cost of housing and transport, a fact confirmed by the Economist Intelligence Unit in 2014, which declared Singapore the world's most expensive city to live in.

night. (www.2amdessertbar.com; 21A Lorong Liput; dishes $15-20; ⏰6pm-2am Mon-Sat; ⓂHolland Village)

Daily Scoop
ICE CREAM $

12 🍴 Map p130, B3

Pimped with whimsical murals, Daily Scoop keeps punters cool with over 40 creative flavours of hand-churned ice cream. Get indecisive over flavours like strawberry shortcake or durian, slurp on a thick milkshake, or fill up on waffles or rich brownies. (www.thedailyscoop. com.sg; 43 Jln Merah Saga; ice cream from $3.50; ⏰11am-10pm Mon-Thu, to 10.30pm Fri & Sat, 2-10pm Sun; ⓂHolland Village)

> ### Understand
> **Tanglin Barracks**
> - - - - - - - - - - - - - - - -
> One of the first barracks constructed in Singapore, Tanglin Barracks (now better known as Dempsey Hill) made its debut in 1861. The original buildings were spacious, elevated wooden structures topped with thatched *attap* (sugar palm) roofs and able to house 50 men. Among the barracks' amenities were hospital wards, wash houses, kitchens, a library, a reading room and a school, as well as officers quarters. Extensive renovation between 1934 and 1936 saw the airy verandahs make way for more interior space, though the French-tiled roofs – which had replaced the original thatched ones decades earlier – were thankfully preserved. Home to the British military for over a century, the barracks served as the headquarters of the Ministry of Defence between 1972 and 1989, before their current reinvention as an upmarket hang-out for lattes, antiques and ladies who lunch.

Drinking

Park
BAR

13 🍸 Map p130, A3

Holland Village's coolest dig sits in converted shipping containers at the top of Holland Ave. Industrial yellow tables, shophouse tiles and filament bulbs deliver a suitably hip fit-out, with outdoor patio seating and well-priced pints for this part of town. Order a side of spam chips, one of life's unexpected surprises. (281 Holland Ave, 01-01; ⏰10am-midnight Tue-Thu & Sun, to 2am Fri & Sat; 🛜; ⓂHolland Village)

RedDot Brewhouse
MICROBREWERY

14 🍸 Map p130, F4

In a quiet spot in Dempsey Hill, RedDot Brewhouse has been pouring its own microbrews for years. Ditch the average food and focus on the suds, sipped to the sound of screeching parrots. There are nine beers on tap (from $6 for a half-pint), including an eye-catching, spirulina-spiked green pilsner. Happy hour runs from noon to 7pm, with $4 half-pints and $8 pints. (www.reddotbrewhouse.com.sg; 25A Dempsey Rd; ⏰noon-midnight Mon-Thu, noon-2am Fri & Sat, 10am-midnight Sun; 🚌7, 75, 77, 105, 106, 123, 174)

Wala Wala Café Bar
BAR

15 🚾 Map p130, A3

Perennially packed at weekends (and on most evenings, in fact), Wala Wala's main draw is its live music on the 2nd floor, with warm-up acts Monday to Friday from 7pm,s and main acts nightly from 9.30pm. Downstairs it pulls in football fans with its large sports screens. Like most of the places here, tables spill out onto the street in the evenings. (www.walawala.sg; 31 Lorong Mambong; ⏰4pm-1am Mon-Thu, 4pm-2am Fri, 3pm-2am Sat, 3pm-1am Sun; Ⓜ Holland Village)

Shopping

Shang Antique
ANTIQUES

16 🔒 Map p130, F4

Specialising in antique religious artefacts from Cambodia, Laos, Thailand, India and Burma, as well as reproductions, there are items in here dating back nearly 2000 years, with price tags to match. Those with more style than savings can pick up anything from old opium pots to beautiful table runners for under $30. (www.shangantique.com.sg; 18D Dempsey Rd; ⏰10.30am-7pm; 🚌7, 75, 77, 105, 106, 123, 174)

Em Gallery
FASHION, HOMEWARES

17 🔒 Map p130, F4

Singapore-based Japanese designer Emiko Nakamura keeps Dempsey's lunching ladies looking fab in her light, sculptural creations. Emiko also collaborates with hilltribes in northern Laos to create naturally dyed handwoven handicrafts. Other homewares might include limited-edition (and reasonably priced) Khmer pottery from Cambodia or handmade Thai dinner sets. (📞6475 6941; www.emtradedesign.com; Block 16, 01-04/05, Dempsey Rd; ⏰10am-7pm Mon-Fri, 11am-7pm Sat & Sun; 🚌7, 75, 77, 105, 106, 123, 174)

Pasardina Fine Living
ANTIQUES, HOMEWARES

18 🔒 Map p130, F4

If you plan on giving your home a tropical Asian makeover, this treasure trove is a good starting point. Inspired by traditional Indonesian design, its collection includes beautiful teak furniture, ceramic and wooden statues, bark lampshades and the odd wooden archway. (13 Dempsey Rd; ⏰9.30am-6.30pm; 🚌7, 75, 77, 105, 106, 123, 174)

Holland Village Shopping Centre
MALL

19 🔒 Map p130, A3

Holland Village Shopping Centre remains a magnet for expats seeking art, handicrafts, homewares and offbeat fashion. Dive into **Lim's Arts & Living**, where tacky giftware sits alongside some genuinely good finds, from Peranakan-style ceramics to *cheongsam* frocks. Shopped out: hit the nail spas on Level 3. (211 Holland Ave; ⏰10am-8.30pm; Ⓜ Holland Village)

Explore

Southwest Singapore

Home to Singapore's epic container terminals, this corner of the city is often overlooked by visitors, who pass through only to take the cable car between Mt Faber and Sentosa. But look closer and you'll find some worthy magnets, among them the spectacular Southern Ridges trail, the elegant NUS Museum and languid, stuck-in-time Colbar.

The Sights in a Day

Start with a quick bite-to-go at **VivoCity** (p147), then slip into **Labrador Nature Reserve** (p145), a slice of tropical forest scattered with wartime relics. If you're lucky, the Labrador Secret Tunnels will have reopened. Alternatively, check out kooky theme park **Haw Par Villa** (p145). Either way, continue further on the MRT Yellow Line to Kent Ridge, from where a shuttle bus leads to **NUS Museum** (p144) and its beautiful artefacts and art.

Hop back on the MRT and get off at Pasir Panjang for cheap chow at **Eng Lock Koo** (p146). From here, amble up to hilltop **Reflections at Bukit Chandu** (p141) to relive the area's bloody past, then step inside adjoining Kent Ridge Park to begin your easy trek along the jungle-fringed **Southern Ridges** (p140) walking trail.

The walk terminates at Mt Faber, where drinks and dinner are served with stunning views at Japanese restaurant **Moonstone** (p146). Alternatively, catch a taxi to languid **Colbar** (p147) for cooling ciders and beers in an old British colonial mess hall.

Top Sights
Southern Ridges (p140)

Best of Singapore
Museums & Galleries
NUS Museum (p144)

Reflections at Bukit Chandu (p141)

Gillman Barracks (p144)

Eating
Tamarind Hill (p145)

PeraMakan (p146)

Shopping
VivoCity (p147)

Getting There

M MRT Southwest Singapore is well served by the MRT. Some attractions have their namesake stations. Otherwise, HarbourFront (Yellow and Purple Lines), Pasir Panjang (Yellow Line), Jurong East (Green and Red Lines) and Kent Ridge (Yellow Line) are useful stations.

Top Sights
Southern Ridges

A series of parks and hills connecting Mt Faber to West Coast Park, the Southern Ridges will have you trekking through the jungle without ever really leaving the city. While the whole route spans 9km, the best stretch is from Kent Ridge Park to Mt Faber. It's relatively easy, and serves up some stunning sights, from lofty skyline and jungle vistas to a seriously striking, wave-like walkway.

Map p142; D3

www.nparks.gov.sg

Ⓜ Pasir Panjang

Henderson Waves walkway

Don't Miss

Reflections at Bukit Chandu

Commemorating the last stand of the Malay Regiment against the Japanese in 1942, **Reflections at Bukit Chandu** (www.nhb.gov.sg; 31K Pepys Rd; adult/child $2/1; ⊙9am-5.30pm Tue-Sun; M Pasir Panjang) combines first-hand accounts, personal artefacts and films to describe the brutal battle that almost wiped out the regiment.

Kent Ridge Park

Behind Reflections you'll find Kent Ridge Park. It's strangely deserted so you'll have its short yet wonderful canopy walk pretty much to yourself. From here, stroll downhill to HortPark.

Forest Walk

From HortPark, a leaf-like bridge crosses over Alexandra Rd, leading to the stunning Forest Walk. While you can opt for the Earth trail, the Elevated Walkway is more appealing, offering eye-level views of the jungle canopy covering Telok Blangah Hill.

Henderson Waves

Further along you'll hit the remarkable Henderson Waves, an undulating sculptural walkway suspended 36m above the forest floor. The towers that seem to rise straight out of the jungle are part of Reflections at Keppel Bay – a residential development designed by world-renowned architect Daniel Libeskind.

Mt Faber

Stretching 166m above the southern fringe of the city, Mt Faber's terraced trails wind past strategically positioned viewpoints. It's here you'll find the cable-car service to HarbourFront and Sentosa.

ALBERT TAN PHOTO/GETTY IMAGES ©

☑ **Top Tips**

▶ The best time to hit the trail is late afternoon. You avoid the worst of the midday heat and can make it to Mt Faber in time for sunset drinks or dinner.

▶ Wear comfortable shoes, sunglasses and a sunhat. If rain is on the cards, bring an umbrella. And always pack plenty of water.

▶ Bring your camera. The walk delivers beautiful views of the city, jungle and South China Sea.

▶ If you encounter monkeys, do not feed them. This only encourages them to pester humans.

✗ **Take a Break**

For drinks and yakitori with stunning island and sea views, head to Moonstone (p146).

For more casual bites, opt for Spuds & Aprons (p146), also atop Mt Faber.

A
Kent Ridge Ⓜ
B NUS Museum
2
C
D

1
National University of Singapore
Ayer Rajah Expwy
Science Park Dr
Portsdown Rd
Portsdown Ave
🚻 10
Queensway

Kent Ridge Park

2
4
Ⓞ Haw Par Villa

Haw Par Villa Ⓜ
Buona Vista South Rd
HortPark
Southern Ⓞ Ridges

3
Pepys Rd
Ⓧ 8
Ⓜ Pasir Panjang
Pepys Rd
West Coast Hwy
Gillman Barracks 3
Alexandra Rd

PASIR PANJANG

4
Labrador Villa Rd
Ⓜ Labrador Park
6 Ⓧ
5 Ⓞ
Port Rd

5
Sebarok Channel
Labrador Nature Reserve

For reviews see	
Ⓞ Top Sights	p140
Ⓞ Sights	p144
Ⓧ Eating	p145
🍷 Drinking	p147
⭐ Entertainment	p147
🛍 Shopping	p147

Ⓝ 0 —————— 500 m
0 —————— 0.25 miles

E F G H

1

Singapore River

Tiong Bahru Rd

Alexandra Rd

Ⓜ Redhill

Delta Stadium

Tiong Bahru Rd

Tiong Bahru Park

🏛 **Jln Bukit Merah**

Henderson Rd

Henderson Park

Lower Delta Rd

Ⓜ Tiong Bahru

2

Ayer Rajah Expwy

Jln Bukit Merah

3

Telok Blangah Hill Park

Henderson Rd

Lower Delta Rd

✕ 9

Mt Faber Park

▲ Mt Faber

Mt Faber Park & Cable Car

1 ◉

4

Telok Blangah Ⓜ

7 ✕

Telok Blangah Rd

Sentosa Gateway

HarbourFront Ⓜ

VivoCity 🔒

12

☆ 11

HarbourFront

Jardine Steps

HarbourFront Cruise & Ferry Terminal

Keppel Harbour

Keppel Island

Sights

Mt Faber Park & Cable Car

PARK

1 Map p142, G4

Mt Faber (116m) is the centrepiece of Mt Faber Park and the climax to the Southern Ridges nature walk. The most spectacular way to get here is via the **cable car** (www.singaporecablecar.com.sg; adult/child return $29/18; ⏱8.45am-9.45pm), which connects Mt Faber to HarbourFront and Sentosa – frustratingly, only return tickets are sold. Alternatively, you can walk. It's a short but steep climb through second-ary rainforest, dotted with lookout posts and some splendid colonial-era black-and-white bungalows. (www.faberpeaksingapore.com; ⏱park 8.45am-10pm; MHarbourFront)

NUS Museum

MUSEUM

2 Map p142, A1

Located on the campus of the National University of Singapore (NUS), this trio of small art museums holds some remarkably fine collections. Ancient Chinese ceramics and bronzes dominate the ground-floor **Lee Kong Chian Art Museum**, while one floor up, the **South and Southeast Asian Gallery** showcases paintings, sculpture and textiles from the region. Above it, the **Ng Eng Teng Gallery** is dedicated to Ng Eng Teng (1934–2001), one of Singapore's foremost artists, best known for his figurative sculptures. (www.nus.edu.sg/museum; 50 Kent Ridge Cres, University Cultural Centre; admission free; ⏱10am-7.30pm Tue-Sat, to 6pm Sun; MKent Ridge, then a university shuttle bus A2)

Gillman Barracks

ART GALLERIES

3 Map p142, D3

Built in 1936 as a British military encampment, Gillman Barracks is now a rambling art outpost, with 15 commercial galleries studding verdant grounds. Among the galleries is New York's **Sundaram Tagore**, whose stable of artists include award-winning photographers Edward Burtynsky and Annie Leibovitz. Alight at Labrador Park MRT station and walk north up

---

Local Life
Kranji Farms

For a refreshingly different take on Singaporean life, consider visiting Singapore's small, thriving cluster of farms. A daily minibus service, the **Kranji Express** (Kranji MRT Station; adult/child $3/1; ⏱9am-6pm, every 75min), does a loop from the Kranji MRT station, visiting many of the best farms en route. One of the best is **Bollywood Veggies** (www.bollywoodveggies.com; 100 Neo Tiew Rd; admission $2, free with Kranji Express tickets; ⏱9am-6.30pm Wed-Fri, 8am-6.30pm Sat & Sun), where you can ramble through rustic gardens planted with cashew, papaya and starfruit trees, and nosh on beautiful, healthy grub at the bistro.

Alexandra Rd for 800m; the entry to Gillman Barracks is on your right. A one-way taxi from the CBD costs around $10. (www.gillmanbarracks.com; 9 Lock Rd; ⊘individual galleries vary, usually 11am-7pm Tue-Sat, to 6pm Sun; Ⓜ Labrador Park)

Haw Par Villa MUSEUM

4 ◉ Map p142, A2

The refreshingly weird and kitsch Haw Par Villa was the brainchild of Aw Boon Haw, the creator of the medicinal salve Tiger Balm. After building a villa here in 1937 for his beloved brother and business partner, Aw Boon Par, the siblings began building a Chinese mythology theme park within the grounds. The result is a curious garden of garish statues and dioramas, each recounting Chinese folk stories and fables. (☑6872 2780; 262 Pasir Panjang Rd; admission free; ⊘9am-7pm, Ten Courts of Hell exhibit 9am-6pm; Ⓜ Haw Par Villa)

Labrador Nature Reserve HISTORICAL PARK

5 ◉ Map p142, D5

Combining forest trails rich in birdlife and a beachfront park, Labrador Park is scattered with evocative war relics, only rediscovered in the 1980s. Look out for old gun emplacements mounted on moss-covered concrete casements as well as for the remains of the entrance to the old fort that stood guard on this hill. The Labrador Secret Tunnels – a fascinating series of

Labrador Nature Reserve

storage and armament bunkers – were closed indefinitely at the time of writing. (www.nparks.gov.sg; Labrador Villa Rd; ⊘24hr; ☐408, Ⓜ Labrador Park)

Eating

Tamarind Hill THAI $$

6 ✕ Map p142, D4

In a colonial bungalow in lush Labrador Park, Tamarind Hill sets an elegant scene for exceptional Thai. The highlight here is the Sunday brunch (noon to 3pm), which offers a buffet of beautiful cold dishes and salads, as well as the ability to order as many dishes off the à la carte menu as you like (the sauteed squid is sublime). Book ahead. (☏6278 6364; www.tamarindrestaurants.com; 30 Labrador Villa Rd; mains $20-59, Sun brunches $60; ☺noon-3pm & 6.30-10.30pm; 🚌408, ᴹLabrador Park)

PeraMakan   PERANAKAN $$

7 🍴 Map p142, E5

Run by a genial pair of cooking enthusiasts, this paragon of homestyle Baba-Nonya cuisine migrated from its spiritual Joo Chiat home. Thankfully, classics such as *sambal* squid and *rendang* (spicy coconut curry) remain as

Local Life
A Public Splash
Singapore has some seriously impressive public pools, which, at a couple of dollars or less, are among the island's best bargains. Top of the list is **Jurong East Sports & Cultural Centre** (☏6563 5052; 21 Jurong East St 31; adult/child $2/1; ☺8am-9.30pm Tue, Thu & Fri; 6.30am-9.30pm Wed & Sat, 2.30-9.30pm Sun; ᴹChinese Garden), a wow-inducing combo of giant wave pool, lazy river, waterslides, wading pool, jacuzzi and Olympic-sized pool. Expect huge crowds on weekends. The centre is a 600m walk from Chinese Garden MRT. Before heading in, double check opening times; visit www.myactivesg.com for more information.

plate-lickingly good as ever. One dish definitely not worth missing is the *ayam buah keluak* (chicken in a rich spicy sauce served with Indonesian black-nut pulp). (www.peramakan.com; 10 Bukit Chermin Rd, L3 Keppel Club; mains $10-24; ☺11.30am-2.30pm & 6-9.30pm; 📶; ᴹTelok Blangah)

Eng Lock Koo   HAWKER CENTRE $

8 🍴 Map p142, B3

Handy for breakfast or lunch if you're on your way to either Reflections at Bukit Chandu or Kent Ridge Park for the Southern Ridges walk, this small collection of stalls inside an airy corner-shop premises does tea and coffee, not to mention hawker favourites like chicken rice and *nasi goreng*. (114 Pasir Panjang Rd, cnr Pepys Rd; mains from $3; ☺individual stalls vary, generally 5am-3pm; ᴹPasir Panjang)

Faber Peak   INTERNATIONAL $$

9 🍴 Map p142, G4

The Mt Faber cable car terminal is home to a trio of eateries, all with bird's-eye views. Top billing goes to patio-graced Japanese yakitori restaurant **Moonstone** (www.epicurean. com.sg; dishes $4-20; ☺4pm-12.30am Sun-Thu, to 2am Fri & Sat). Cross-cultural dishes and patio dining define **Faber Bistro** (☏6377 9688; www.mountfaber. com.sg; mains $13-15; ☺3-11pm Mon-Thu, to 2am Fri, 11am-2am Sat, 11am-11pm Sun), while family-friendly **Spuds & Aprons** (☏6377 9688; mains $16-38; ☺11am-11pm Sun-Wed, to 12.30am Thu, to 2am Fri & Sat) is another global affair, with a mix of local dishes, sandwiches and mains such as juicy pork belly. (☎6377 9688; www.faberpeaksingapore.com; 109 Mt Faber Rd; Ⓜ HarbourFront, 🚠 Mount Faber)

Drinking

Colbar   BAR

10 🍺 Map p142, C1

Raffish Colbar is an evocative colonial throwback, a former British officers mess turned languid drinking spot. It's still 1930-something here: a place where money is kept in a drawer, football team photos hang on the wall and locals linger with beers and well-priced ciders on the spacious verandah. (☎6779 4859; 9A Whitchurch Rd; ⏰11am-midnight Tue-Sun, kitchen closes 8.30pm; 🚌191)

Entertainment

St James Power Station   CLUB VENUE

11 ⭐ Map p142, H5

What was once a 1920s coal-fired power station is now a multivenue entertainment hub. Popular with a mostly local crowd, its interconnected bars and clubs include lush bar **Peppermint Park** (⏰5pm-3am Mon-Thu, to 4am Fri & Sat), thumping Thai club-live-music hybrid **Neverland II** (⏰9.30pm-6am) and karaoke bar **Mono** (⏰6pm-5am Sun-

Thu, to 6am Fri & Sat). Minimum age at Mono is 18, while at Neverland II it's 21 for women and 23 for men. (www.stjamespowerstation.com; 3 Sentosa Gateway Ⓜ HarbourFront)

Shopping

VivoCity   MALL

12 🔒 Map p142, H5

More than just Singapore's largest shopping mall, VivoCity offers that rare commodity: open space. There's an outdoor kids' playground on Level 2 and a rooftop 'skypark' where little ones can splash about in free-to-use paddling pools. The retail mix is predominately midrange, and there's a large Golden Village cineplex. (www.vivocity.com.sg; 1 HarbourFront Walk; ⏰10am-10pm; Ⓜ HarbourFront)

The Best of
Singapore

Cloud Forest dome, Gardens by the Bay (p29)
HEINRICH VAN DEN BERG/GETTY IMAGES ©

t Walks
onial
gapore

🏃 The Walk

In a city firmly fixed on the future, the Colonial District offers a rare, precious glimpse of a romanticised era and its architectural legacies. This is the Singapore of far-flung missionaries and churches, Palladian-inspired buildings, high-society cricket clubs and the legendary Raffles Hotel. This walk takes in some of the city's most beautiful heritage buildings, swaths of soothing greenery, spectacular skyline views and even a spot of contemporary Asian art. Time it to coincide with a postwalk lunch or dinner by the Singapore River.

Start Singapore Art Museum; Ⓜ Bras Basah

Finish MICA; Ⓜ Clarke Quay

Length 2km; two hours with stops

🍴 Take a Break

End your saunter with trademark chilli crab at Jumbo Seafood (p37).

Singapore Art Museum

❶ Singapore Art Museum

The **Singapore Art Museum** (p32) occupies a former Catholic boys school. Original features include the shuttered windows, ceramic floor tiles and inner quadrangle. The central dome and sweeping arcade portico were early-20th-century additions.

❷ Raffles Hotel

Head southeast along Bras Basah Rd, passing the Renaissance-inspired **Cathedral of the Good Shepherd**, and the English Gothic **CHIJMES**, a convent-turned-restaurant complex. Diagonally opposite CHIJMES is the legendary **Raffles Hotel** (p32).

❸ St Andrew's

You'll find wedding-cake **St Andrew's Cathedral** (p35) further south on North Bridge Rd. Completed in 1838, it was torn down after being struck by lightning (twice!), and rebuilt by Indian convicts in 1862. It's one of Singapore's few surviving examples of English Gothic architecture.

④ City Hall

Built in 1928, **City Hall** is where Lord Louis Mountbatten announced Japanese surrender in 1945 and Lee Kuan Yew declared Singapore's independence in 1965. City Hall and the Old Supreme Court, built in 1939, house the **National Gallery Singapore** (p32).

⑤ Padang

Opposite City Hall is the open field of the **Padang**, home to the Singapore Cricket Club and Singapore Recreation Club. It was here that the invading Japanese herded the European community together before marching them off to Changi Prison.

⑥ Victoria Theatre

Below where St Andrew's Rd curves to the left stand a group of colonial-era buildings, including the **Victoria Theatre & Concert Hall**. Completed in 1862, it was originally the Town Hall. It was also one of Singapore's first Victorian Revivalist buildings.

⑦ MICA

Hang a right to hit the Singapore River. The multicoloured building on the corner of Hill St is the old Hill St Police Station. Dubbed a 'sky-scraper' when built in 1934, it's now known as **MICA** (p36) and home to a string of contemporary art galleries.

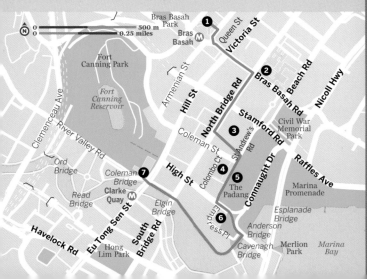

Best Walks
New-Millennium Singapore

The Walk

Singapore is not marching towards the future – it is inventing it. Drunk on ambition, the city has been diligently revamping itself with a bold new wave of quirky, edgy and sometimes controversial developments. This walk will see you exploring the very heart of the 'new Singapore', Marina Bay, a daring precinct where cultural buildings echo fruits and flowers, where bridges recall DNA strings, and where botanic gardens look straight off the set of *The Day of the Triffids*. Welcome to tomorrow.

Start Esplanade – Theatres on the Bay; Ⓜ Esplanade

Finish Gardens by the Bay; Ⓜ Bayfront

Length 2km; three hours with stops

Take a Break

End your time travel with sustainable fine dining at Pollen (p39) or street food classics at breezy hawker centre Satay by the Bay (p39).

Helix Bridge

❶ Esplanade – Theatres by the Bay

Singapore's head-turning **Esplanade – Theatres on the Bay** (p44) features a theatre and concert hall under two superstructures of double-glazed laminated glass and aluminium sunshades. Designed by Singapore's DP Architects and London's Michael Wilford & Partners, its price-tag was a cool $600 million.

❷ Helix Bridge

Walk east along Marina Promenade to the 280m-long **Helix Bridge**. It's the world's first double-helix bridge, designed by Australia's Cox Architecture and Singapore's Architects 61. Viewing platforms offer an impressive vantage point for photos across to Collyer Quay, Merlion and Fullerton buildings.

❸ ArtScience Museum

The white, lotuslike building on the other side of the bridge is the **ArtScience Museum** (p35). Opened in 2011, the structure is the work of Israeli-born architect Moshe Safdie. The building consists of 10 finger-like strcutures capped by skylights, lighting the galleries within. Beside the museum is the world's first floating **Louis Vuitton** store.

❹ Marina Bay Sands

Both the ArtScience Museum and the Louis Vuitton store form part of the ambitious **Marina Bay Sands** integrated resort, home to the lavish **Shoppes at Marina Bay Sands** (p46) and a gravity-defying cantilevered skydeck. Known as the 'SkyPark', the deck is large enough to park four-and-a-half A380s. Catch the lift to **Ku Dé Ta** for a breathtaking vista.

❺ Gardens by the Bay

From Marina Bay Sands, a pedestrian overpass leads you to **Gardens by the Bay** (p28), a 21st-century park housing the world's largest conservatories, an aerial walkway and state-of-the-art Supertrees whose trunks contain solar hot water and photovoltaic collectors, rainwater harvesting devices and venting ducts.

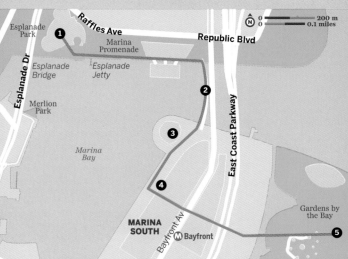

Best
Tours

Best Neighbourhood Tours

Original Singapore Walks (☎6325 1631; www.singaporewalks.com; adult $35-55, child $15-30) Engaging walking tours, with themes such as Chinatown, Little India, Kampong Glam and the Quays. No booking required; simply check the website for meeting places and times.

Real Singapore Tours (☎6247 7340; www.betelbox.com/singapore-tours.htm; 200 Joo Chiat Rd; tours $80-$100) Choose from nature walks, coastline cycling or food odysseys (usually at 6pm on Thursday) through ro the historic Joo Chiat neighbourhood.

Chinatown Trishaw Night Tour (www.viator.com; adult/child $72/47) Atmospheric, four-hour tour of Chinatown including dinner, a trishaw ride and bumboat (motorised sampan) cruise along the Singapore River.

Trishaw Uncle (www.trishawuncle.com.sg; Queen St; 30min tour adult/child from $39/29, 45min 49/39) Hop on a trishaw for a 45-minute exploration of Bugis and Little India. You'll find the trishaw terminal on Queen St, between the Fu Lu Shou Complex and Albert Centre Market and Food Centre.

Best Water Tours

Singapore River Cruise (☎6336 6111; www.rivercruise.com.sg; adult/child $22/12; ⊙9am-11pm; MClarke Quay) Jump on a traditional bumboat and sail up and down the Singapore River on these 40- and 60-minute tours through the central city.

Duck Tours (☎6338 6877; www.ducktours.com.sg; Nicoll Hwy, 01-330, Suntec City Mall; adult/child $33/23; ⊙10am-6pm; MEsplanade) Head out on a remodelled WWII amphibious Vietnamese war craft for a surprisingly informative, engaging one-hour tour that traverses land and water.

SENG CHYE TEO/GETTY IMAGES ©

The route focuses on Marina Bay and the Colonial District.

Best Tours with a Twist

Jeffery Tan (☎9784 6848; http://jefflimo.tripod.com/jefflimo.htm) 'Singapore's Singing Cabbie' can croon in nine languages and will happily serenade you while showing you the sights of your choice. Tan also offers a food tour and video karaoke in the limo.

Bukit Brown Tour (www.bukitbrown.com) Free, fascinating walking tours through one of Singapore's most historic, wild and beautiful cemeteries, currently under threat from development. Check the website for upcoming tour dates and times.

Best
Festivals

Hungry Chinese ghosts, fire-walking Hindu faithful, international indie-rock gigs: Singapore's social calendar is intensely eclectic, reflecting both its multicultural make-up and an insatiable determination to shake off its staid, uptight image. It's working, with annual staples including the world's first F1 night race and Australian indie-music Laneway Festival.

ANDREW JK TAN/GETTY IMAGES ©

Best Hindu Festivals

Thaipusam (January) *Kavadis* (heavy metal frames) pierce parading devotees.

Deepavali (October) Little India glows for the 'Festival of Lights'.

Thimithi (November) Hindus walk over white-hot coals at Sri Mariamman Temple.

Best for Musos

Laneway Festival (http://singapore.lanewayfestival.com.au) Uberhip indie-music fest; January.

Singapore International Jazz Festival (www.sing-jazz.com) Four-day showcase of established and emerging jazz talent; January.

Mosaic Music Festival (www.mosaicmusicfestival.com) World music, jazz and indie acts; March.

Singapore International Festival of Arts (www.sifa.sg) Music, dance, drama and art; August.

Best Chinese Festivals

Chinese New Year (February) Dragon dances, fireworks, food and spectacular street decorations.

Hungry Ghost Festival (August) Fires, food and Chinese opera honour roaming spirits.

Best for Foodies

Singapore Food Festival (www.yoursingapore.com) Ten days of tastings, dinners and food-themed tours; July.

Mooncake Festival (August/September) Lanterns light up Chinatown as revellers feast on mooncakes.

Best Only-in-Singapore Festivals

Chingay (www.chingay.org.sg) Singapore's biggest street party, held on the 22nd day after Chinese New Year; February.

Singapore National Day (www.ndp.org.sg) Extravagant processions and fireworks. Snap tickets up well in advance; 9 August.

Formula One Night Race (www.f1singapore.com) After-dark F1 racing on a spectacular Marina Bay street circuit; September.

Best
Shopping

TIM BEWER/GETTY IMAGES ©

Bangkok and Hong Kong might upstage it on the bargain front, but when it comes to choice, few cities match Singapore. Whether you're after Gucci mules, fashion-forward local threads or a 16th-century temple artefact, you'll have little trouble bagging it in Singapore's decadent malls, progressive boutiques and cluttered heirloom businesses.

Shopping Roadmap

While mall-heavy, fashion-centric Orchard Rd is Singapore's retail queen, it's only one of several retail hubs. For computers and electronics, hit specialist electronics malls like Funan DigitaLife and Sim Lim Square. Good places for antiques include Tanglin Shopping Centre, Dempsey Hill and Chinatown. For fabrics and textiles, scour Little India and Kampong Glam. Kampong Glam is also famous for its perfume traders and boutique-lined Haji Lane. For in-the-know independent labels, design objects and books, explore Tiong Bahru.

Bagging a Bargain

While Singapore is no longer the electronics nirvana it used to be, it can offer a few savings for those who do their homework. Know the price of things before you start shopping around and always ask vendors what they can do to 'sweeten the deal'; they should at least be able to throw in a camera case or some memory cards. Sim Lim Square is well known for its range and negotiable prices, but also for taking the uninitiated for a ride: a quick Google search will bring up blacklisted businesses. Rival Funan DigitaLife Mall has similar prices, but the businesses are generally considered more trustworthy. A vendor should always provide the warranty in store.

☑ **Top Tip**

▶ To ensure a good deal on electronics, know the prices back home, and always compare prices at a number of competing businesses.

Best Souvenirs

Raffles Hotel Arcade
Pick up anything from vintage posters to city tomes at the all-budgets Raffles Hotel Gift Shop. (p45)

Tyrwhitt General Company Cool, unique objects designed and made in Singapore. (p109)

Little Shophouse Hand-beaded shoes, ceramics and other Peranakan gifts. (p109)

ION Orchard Mall

Sifr Aromatics Bespoke fragrances and vintage perfume bottles. (p109)

Best Luxury Malls

ION Orchard Mall High-end labels in Singapore's most striking mall. (p59)

Shoppes at Marina Bay Sands Bayside luxury and the world's first floating Louis Vuitton store. (p46)

Paragon Coveted brands and a dedicated children's floor. (p60)

Best Midrange Malls

313@Somerset Midrange staples and an upbeat vibe. (p59)

ION Orchard Mall Everything from H&M to Uniqlo and Zara. (p59)

VivoCity High street labels galore at Singapore's biggest mall. (p147)

Best Tech

Funan DigitaLife Mall Six floors of electronics, cameras and computers. (p46)

Sim Lim Square Bargain-price electronics for seasoned hagglers. (p111)

Best Local & Independent Fashion

Front Row Cognoscenti labels and accessories from Asia and beyond. (p45)

Reckless Shop Imaginative creations by the talented Afton Chan. (p60)

Nana & Bird Feminine fashion from local and emerging foreign designers. (p63)

Willow and Huxley A petite boutique with a big reputation for clued-in local and foreign threads. (p84)

Best Antiques

Antiques of the Orient A treasure trove of old Asian books, prints and maps. (p60)

Shang Antique Rummage for ancient Asian artefacts in tranquil Dempsey Hill. (p137)

Best
Street Food

It's one of Singapore's great pleasures: ambling into a lively hawker centre in your flip-flops, navigating the steam, smoke and chatter of the stalls, then kicking back with a cold beer and a dirt-cheap feast of mouth-watering regional dishes. And the thrifty feasting doesn't end there, with enough old-school *kopitiams* (coffeeshops) and foodie-approved food courts to keep both tastebuds and wallets purring.

JACK HOLLINGSWORTH/GETTY IMAGES ©

Stalls, Malls & Queues

When it comes to local grub, it's hard to beat Singapore's hawker centres. These large complexes of Chinese, Malay, Indonesian and Indian food stalls are the happiest consequence of the city's cultural stew. They're also great for a cheap feed, with most dishes costing between $3 and $6. If you insist on air-con, head to Singapore's equally famous mall food courts. Unlike their Western counterparts, they peddle fresh, authentic grub for some of the world's pickiest tastebuds. Wherever you go, join the longest queue. While stalls go in and out of favour very quickly, in-the-know Singaporeans are always happy to line up for 30 minutes to savour the very best.

Hawker Centres Decoded

You're at a hawker centre. Now what? Locals always set up base camp before going in search of food. Plonk down a member of your group at a table, or lay a packet of tissues on a seat. If there are no free tables, it's normal to share with strangers. Table reserved, hit the food stalls. If they bear a 'self-service' sign, you'll have to wait and carry the food back to your table. Other stalls will ask for your table number and deliver the order to you.

Best Hawker Grub

Maxwell Road Hawker Centre Popular, accessible and famed for its Hainanese chicken rice. (p76)

Chinatown Complex Sprawling labyrinth with legendary dry *bee hoon* (vermicelli noodles). (p76)

Gluttons Bay Lipsmacking hawker fare and a festive vibe on Marina Bay. (p37)

Satay by the Bay Fragrant satay and other sizzling classics at sci-fi Gardens by the Bay. (p152)

Malaysian Food Street Legendary Malaysian hawker stalls right beside Universal Studios. (p120)

Hawker food

Best Food Courts

Takashimaya Food Village Basement wonderland of Japanese, Korean and other Asian delicacies. (p56)

Food Republic Hawker-style classics and restaurant-style nooks atop an Orchard Rd mall. (p54)

Rasapura Masters Street food from Asia and beyond inside ostentatious Marina Bay Sands. (p39)

Best Snacks

Tong Heng Veteran pastry shop with sweet and savoury treats from southern China. (p78)

Moghul Sweet Shop Take-away Indian sweets in every colour of the rainbow. (p106)

Kim Choo Kueh Chang Bite-sized Peranakan treats in an old-school Katong bakery. (p87)

Best Kopitiams

Ya Kun Kaya Toast Historic hang-out serving Singapore's best runny eggs and *kaya* (coconut jam) toast. (p77)

Killiney Kopitiam Another top spot for old-school Singaporean breakfasts, plus solid curries, laksa and *nasi lemak*. (p54)

Best Malay & Indonesian

Warong Nasi Pariaman Veteran *nasi padang* (Malay rice and the accompanying meat and vegetable dishes) stall with a cultish following. (p103)

Satay Street Sizzling satay, cold beer and alfresco tables on a blocked-off CBD street. (p77)

Zam Zam Fresh, epic *murtabak* in the shadow of the golden-domed Sultan Mosque. (p105)

Best Indian

Gandhi Restaurant Flavour-packed thali, *dosa* and *uttapam* bites. (p103)

Tekka Centre Wriggling produce, saris and city-famous *murtabak* – stuffed savoury pancakes. (p106)

Best
Dining

Beyond the cheap, wham-bam thrills of hawker centres and food courts is a burgeoning scene of solid restaurants in both the midrange and top-end categories. Options are endless: bolt-hole sushi bars in Orchard Rd malls, Southeast Asian fusion and cocktails in Chinatown, even a haute-cuisine French hotspot 70 floors above the city.

MING THEIN / MINGTHEIN.COM/GETTY IMAGES ©

An Evolving Scene

From London chef Jason Atherton's Pollen to New Yorker Mario Batali's Pizzeria Mozza, Singapore has an ever-expanding legion of top-notch, celebrity-chef nosheries. Iggy's remains one of Asia's most coveted destination restaurants, with French chef Julien Royer's Jaan providing lofty competition. Most exciting is Singapore's new breed of lively, midrange eateries, which alongside trailblazers like Kilo, deliver sharp, produce-driven menus in an altogether more relaxed setting. Among the best are Southeast Asian Ding Dong and Mexican Lucha Loco, two of a string of newcomers that have transformed Chinatown and Tanjong Pagar into dining hotspots.

Word on the Street

In Singapore, everyone is a food critic and getting consensus between locals on the best places to chomp is tougher than getting agreement on climate change at the UN. For high-end restaurant news and reviews, visit sg.dining.asiatatler.com. More reviews and headlines await at www.burpple.com/sg. Some local food blogs are also insightful, among them www.ieatishootipost.sg, www.bibikgourmand.blogspot.com and www.ladyironchef.com.

☑ **Top Tip**

▶ Tipping is unnecessary in Singapore, as most restaurants impose a 10% service charge – and nobody ever tips in hawker centres. That said, many do leave a discretionary tip for superlative service at higher-end restaurants.

Best for Romancing

Cliff Secluded fine dining in an enchanting Sentosa setting. (p120)

Jaan Cutting-edge French, high above the Colonial District. (p37)

Iggy's Show-stopping East-meets-West re-inventions on Orchard Rd. (p53)

Halia Ginger-spiked menus in a tropical botanical wonderland. (p133)

Best Crab

Momma Kong's Good deals, huge buns and Singapore's freshest Sri Lankan crabs. (p75)

No Signboard Seafood Superlative white pepper crab in red-light Geylang. (p89)

Jumbo Seafood Classic chilli crab by the Singapore River. (p150)

Best Western & Fusion

Kilo Strictly seasonal Italo-Japanese at an off-the-radar locale. (p36)

Lucha Loco Sucker-punch Mexican and a party vibe off Chinatown. (p75)

Cicheti Market-fresh produce and wood-fired pizza in Kampong Glam. (p103)

Buona Terra Authentic, high-end regional Italian off Orchard Rd. (p56)

Ding Dong Vibrant Southeast Asian twists and matching cocktails. (p73)

Best Chinese & Peranakan

Din Tai Fung Smart, respected chain famed for superlative *xiao long bao* (soup dumplings). (p53)

Tim Ho Wan Hong Kong's most famous dumpling peddler, on Orchard Rd. (p54)

PeraMakan Spicy Peranakan flavours in a resort-like locale. (p146)

Chopsuey Revamped retro Chinese in a colonial-chic setting. (p132)

Nan Hwa Chong Fish-Head Steamboat Corner Singapore's top Teochew-style fish-head steamboat. (p104)

Blue Ginger A still-trendy restaurant with complex Nonya dishes. (p75)

Best Indonesian & Indian

Lagnaa Barefoot Dining Choose-your-own-spice-level adventures. (p101)

Tambuah Mas Authentic, made-from-scratch Indonesian on Orchard Rd. (p54)

Gandhi Restaurant Flavour-packed thali,

dosa and *uttapam* bites in a lo-fi setting. (p103)

Best Brunch

Tamarind Hill Extraordinary Sunday Thai in a jungle-fringed setting. (p145)

Symmetry Decadent dishes and winning coffee in boho Kampong Glam. (p105)

Kith Cafe Lazy, trendy brunching on the Sentosa waterfront. (p120)

Wild Honey Trendy shoppers tucking into all-day breakfasts from around the globe. (p54)

PS Cafe Beautiful produce, lunching ladies and a tropical-chic vibe in Dempsey Hill. (p132)

Best for Old-School Singapore

Colbar Hainanese-style western classics in a former officers mess in western Singapore. (p147)

Killiney Kopitiam Old-school kaya toast and *kopi* a quick walk from Orchard Rd. (p54)

Yet Con Aunties, retro Laminex and Singapore's best Hainanese Chicken Rice. (p39)

Best
For Kids

Safe, clean, respectable Singapore would make an admirable babysitter. From interactive museum galleries and tactile animal sanctuaries to an island packed with blockbuster theme-park thrills, in Singapore young ones are rarely an afterthought, with enough activities and exhibitions to thrill kids of all ages and inclinations. Children are welcome almost anywhere... and fawned over enthusiastically. If you're after a little quality family time, Singapore has you covered.

SHIRLYN LOO/GETTY IMAGES ©

Sentosa: Pleasure Island

While kid-friendly attractions are spread out across Singapore, you'll find the greatest concentration on the island of Sentosa. Here you'll find the LA-style Universal Studios theme park, not to mention a long list of supporting attractions, from splash-happy Adventure Cove Waterpark to zip-lining and Segway tours. You'll need at least a full day to experience everything Sentosa has to offer, not to mention a well-stocked wallet, as most activities, rides and shows cost extra.

Discounts

Kids receive up to 50% discount at most tourist venues. Those under six enjoy free entry to many of Singapore's top museums, including the National Museum of Singapore, Asian Civilisations Museum and Peranakan Museum. Kids under 0.9m tall can ride the MRT for free. Full-time students with photo ID cards also enjoy discounts at many attractions.

☑ **Top Tip**

▶ When visiting Sentosa, be sure to pick up a Sentosa Island map leaflet, available at booths as you enter the island.

Best Museums

National Museum of Singapore Evocative reconstructions, multimedia displays and child-friendly signage take the boring out of history for kids aged six and up. (p24)

Peranakan Museum Child-specific activities, audio stories and colourful artefacts keep little ones engaged at this intriguing museum. (p32)

Asian Civilisations Museum Dress up, play instruments or 'prepare a traditional meal' at the museum's four hands-on Explor-Asian zones. (p26)

MINT Museum of Toys A jaw-dropping, technicolor collection of over 50,000 rare, collectable toys from around the globe. (p35)

Singapore Art Museum Top-notch art complete with periodic kids' activities. (p32)

Best Thrills & Spills

Universal Studios Hollywood-inspired rides, roller coasters and shows for the young and young-at-heart. (p114)

Adventure Cove Waterpark Waterslides, wave pool and Southeast Asia's first hydro-magnetic coaster. (p117)

iFly Plummet a virtual 9000ft without a plane in sight at this indoor skydiving centre. (p118)

Wave House Surf serious waves without ever leaving the pool on Sentosa. (p118)

Singapore Flyer Reach the skies onboard Asia's tallest observation wheel. (p35)

Songs of the Sea Lights, lasers and a stirring score define this multimillion-dollar spectacular. (p121)

Pinnacle@Duxton Affordable, family-friendly skypark with breathtaking city views and green oases. (p75)

Best for Green Adventures

Gardens by the Bay Space-age bio-domes, crazy Supertrees and a children's garden with wet-play zones and tree houses. (p28)

Southern Ridges Walk above the jungle and look out for monkeys. (p140)

Pulau Ubin Hop on a bike and cycle through forest and past colourful shacks on this stuck-in-time island. (p90)

Best Eateries

Rasapura Masters A plethora of food stalls beside an indoor skating rink. (p39)

Casa Verde Family-friendly restaurant in the lush, tropical wonderland of the Botanic Gardens. (p133)

Maxwell Road Hawker Centre Cheap, no-fuss street food with a lively, casual vibe. (p76)

Daily Scoop Over 40 dreamy flavours of hand-churned ice cream. (p136)

Best Animal Watching

Singapore Zoo Breakfast with orang-utans at one of the world's role-model zoological gardens. (p123)

Night Safari Spend the evening with leopards, lions and Himalayan blue sheep at this atmospheric wildlife oasis. (p125)

Butterfly Park & Insect Kingdom Coo and wince over beautiful, endangered and dangerous critters. (p119)

Best
Drinking

From pea-infused Jolly Green Giants at Tippling Club to Singaporean microbrews at The Good Beer Stall and seasonal espresso at Chye Seng Huat Hardware, Singapore is discovering the finer points of drinking. Whatever your poison, you're bound to score: locavore cocktails in a Boat Quay speakeasy, craft beers in a sky-high microbrewery or beachside mojitos on Sentosa.

WILLIAM CHO/GETTY IMAGES ©

Cut-Price Drinks

Singapore is an expensive city to drink in. A beer at most city bars will set you back between $10 and $18, with cocktails commonly ringing in between $20 and $30. That said, many bars offer decent happy-hour deals, typically stretching from around 5pm to 8pm or 9pm, and offering two drinks for the price of one or cheaper 'housepours'. On Wednesdays, Ladies' Night promotions offer cheaper (sometimes free) drinks to women. And if you don't mind plastic tables and fluorescent lights, you can always hang out with the locals at hawker centres and coffeeshops, swilling $6 bottles of Tiger.

Coffee Evolution

While old-school *kopitiams* (coffeeshops) have been serving *kopi* (local coffee) for generations, Singapore's speciality coffee scene is a more recent phenomenon. Inspired by Australia's artisanal coffee culture, contemporary cafes like Plain and Artisan are brewing ethically sourced, seasonal beans, using either espresso machines or 'Third Wave' brewing techniques like Japanese syphons and AeroPress. Also on the increase are cafes sourcing and roasting their own beans, the best of which include Chye Seng Huat Hardware.

Best for Cocktails

Tippling Club Boundary-pushing libations in booming Tanjong Pagar. (p78)

Bitters & Love Custom-made libations in a back-room bar minutes from Boat Quay. (p40)

28 HongKong St Chronological cocktails in an unmarked lounge off Boat Quay. (p41)

Jekyll & Hyde Surprising ingredients and clever twists in up-and-coming Tras St. (p78)

Best for Wine

Ô Batignolles French flair and rotating boutique drops on see-and-be-seen Club St. (p80)

Rooftop bar, 1-Altitude

Best for Beers

Level 33 Slurp brewed-on-site beers 33 floors above the city. (p41)

The Good Beer Company A rotating cast of craft brews in a Chinatown hawker centre. (p79)

BluJaz Café Swill suds to the sound of live sax and strings. (p108)

RedDot Brewhouse Local microbrews in a lush Dempsey setting. (p136)

Best Heritage Settings

Raffles Hotel Sip a Sling where Somerset Maughan once slumbered. (p42)

Colbar Knock back beers at a nostalgic colonial mess in the city's west. (p147)

Black Swan Swill martinis in a deco-licious CBD bar-cum-lounge. (p79)

Emerald Hill Rd Post-shopping drinks on a heritage street off Orchard Rd. (p58)

Best for a View

New Asia Urbane cocktail sessions, 71 floors above the traffic. (p42)

Orgo Cinematic skyline view and a rooftop garden at Esplanade – Theatres on the Bay. (p41)

Breeze Gaze out over red Chinatown rooftops and CBD towers. (p80)

1-Altitude Flirt with vertigo at the world's highest alfresco bar. (p80)

Lantern Stylish rooftop bar with a dazzling centrepiece pool. (p40)

Best for Coffee

Chye Seng Huat Hardware Superlative espresso, filter coffee and on-site roasting. (p109)

Nylon Coffee Roasters Outstanding cafe-roaster hidden in a HDB complex. (p78)

Common Man Coffee An Australian-style cafe and roaster off Robertson Quay. (p38)

Artistry Kicking coffee meets art and culture in eclectic Kampong Glam. (p106)

Maison Ikkoku Third Wave brews and eclectic interiors in Kampong Glam. (p106)

Best
Entertainment

Singapore's nightlife calender is generally booked solid. There's live music, theatre and adrenalin-pumping activities year-round, while at certain times of the year the Red Dot explodes into a flurry of car racing, cultural festivals and hot-ticket music events. Then, when it all gets too much, Singapore's spas are waiting in the wings.

RICHARD I'ANSON/GETTY IMAGES ©

Live Music

Music buffs will find a small, kicking local scene, along with world-class music festivals such as January's indie showcase Laneway Festival, February's Singapore International Jazz Festival, and March's world-music fest Mosaic. Esplanade – Theatres on the Bay hosts free concerts, while the Chinese Theatre Circle performs traditional Chinese opera. A growing number of international pop/rock acts tour Singapore.

Club Culture

Although its future was uncertain at the time this guide was researched, Zouk remains the city's best-known club, with newer hotspots including Japanese-inspired club-lounge Kyō. Dance clubs proliferate in the Clarke Quay area, among them Attica. Check out Super 0 (www.super0.sg), which runs pop-up dance parties. For updated listings, hit www.timeoutsingapore.com/clubs or e-clubbing.com.

The Singapore Stage

Expect quality local and overseas drama at August's Singapore International Festival of Arts and regular dance and drama at Esplanade – Theatres on the Bay. Independent theatre groups like Singapore Repertory Theatre and Theatreworks deliver new works and international adaptations, while Marina Bay Sands hosts Broadway musicals.

☑ **Top Tip**

▶ Check what's on and buy tickets online at www.sistic.com.sg. Expect to pay from $20 to $70 for a ticket to a local theatre production, $90 to $200 for international music acts, and $65 to $200 for big-budget musicals. Gigs by local music acts at local nightspots are often free.

Best for Live Music

BluJaz Café Consistently good jazz and blues in an eclectic Kampong Glam pub. (p108)

Timbrè @ The Substation Local bands and singer-songwriters in the Colonial District. (p45)

Esplanade – Theatres on the Bay Polished performances spanning classical to rock, from Singapore and beyond. (p44)

Crazy Elephant A veteran of the scene, with solid rock and blues from local and visiting talent. (p45)

Hood Up-and-coming venue with regular performances from in-demand local band Timmy. (p108)

Prince of Wales Lively Aussie pub with garage-style bands strumming out mostly acoustic tunes. (p107)

Best Clubs

Zouk World-class DJs and weekly nights spanning retro to electronica. (p43)

Kyō A Japanese-inspired club in a one-time bank in the CBD. (p83)

Attica Multiple venues and music styles, and a flirty crowd in party hub Clarke Quay. (p44)

Best for Drama Queens

Esplanade – Theatres on the Bay World-class productions, from off-Broadway plays to children's theatre. (p44)

Singapore Repertory Theatre A world-class repertoire that includes seasonal Shakespeare at Fort Canning Park. (p45)

Wild Rice Reinterpreted classics, brand new works and striking sets define one of Singapore's top independent companies. (p108)

Best for Chinese Opera

Chinese Theatre Circle Chinese opera meets dinner and a discussion of the art form. (p83)

Bian's Cafe Beijing opera tunes and a bite-sized Chinese opera museum. (p108)

Best LGBT Venues

Tantric Alfresco seating, pop diva chart hits and a flirtatious, mainly male crowd. (p82)

Taboo Singapore's main queer dance club, complete with gym-buff show-offs and crowded late-week dance floor. (p83)

Best
Views & Vistas

Admit it: posting hot travel shots online to torture friends is fun. And while it might surprise you, Singapore makes the perfect partner in crime. From dramatic skyline panoramas to close-up shots of brightly coloured shutters, market produce and lurid tropical flora, the city is ridiculously photogenic. So take aim, shoot and expect no shortage of gratifying Likes.

STEPHEN STUDD/GETTY IMAGES ©

Best Skyline Vistas

New Asia Spectacular Singapore River panorama; whitewashed colonial buildings northside, CBD towers southside. (p42)

1-Altitude The world's tallest alfresco bar in the heart of the CBD. (p80)

Pinnacle@Duxton A panoramic sweep of shophouses, skyscrapers and cargo from atop the world's tallest public housing complex. (p75)

Orgo Breathtaking skyscraper views from the rooftop bar at Esplanade – Theatres on the Bay. (p41)

Best for Architecture Buffs

Gardens by the Bay High-tech trees, bio-domes and striking sculptures. (p28)

Esplanade – Theatres on the Bay Bold and controversial, Singapore's 'giant durian' delivers countless dramatic angles. (p44)

Chinatown Ornate heritage shophouses and old, smokey temples. (p64)

Marina Bay Sands A three-tower sci-fi fantasy with a cantilevered skydeck. (p46)

Emerald Hill Rd An evocative mix of lantern-lit shophouses and elegant, early-20th-century residences. (p52)

Best Is-This-Really-Singapore? Backdrops

Little India Technicolor facades, shrines and garland stalls, mini mountains of spice and dazzling saris. (p92)

Kampong Glam An *Arabian Nights* fantasy of late-night *shisha* cafes, intricate Persian rugs and a storybook, golden-domed mosque. (p92)

Pulau Ubin Tin-roof shacks, free-roaming farm animals and rambling jungle wilderness channel a Singapore long since lost. (p90)

Geylang Rd, Geylang An after-dark otherworld of neon-lit karaoke bars, *kopitiams* and seedy side streets of temples and hookers. (p88)

Best
For Free

KEVIN CLOGSTOUN/GETTY IMAGES ©

Believe it or not, it is possible to savour some of Singapore's top offerings without reaching for your wallet. Whether you're into ancient artefacts, contemporary art, million-dollar lightshows or live-music gigs, you're bound to find it, free of charge. And then there's the simple pleasure of hitting the city's older, colour-saturated neighbourhoods, where daily life is the best show in town.

Best Always-Free Museums

Baba House One of Singapore's best-preserved Peranakan dwellings. (p72)

NUS Museum Three well-curated galleries showcasing ancient and modern Asian art and artefacts. (p144)

Changi Museum & Chapel A moving tribute to Singapore's darkest wartime chapter. (p91)

Best Sometimes-Free Museums

National Museum of Singapore Enjoy free entry to the museum's Living History galleries daily from 6pm to 8pm. (p24)

Singapore Art Museum One of Singapore's art museums, free between 6pm and 9pm on Friday. (p32)

Best Free Art Galleries

Gillman Barracks Top-tier private international galleries from cities like New York and Berlin at a former British military barracks. (p144)

MICA Building Riverside gallery complex showcasing contemporary Asian talent. (p36)

Chan Hampe Galleries One of several galleries in the Raffles Hotel Arcade exhibiting respected local and regional artists. (p45)

Utterly Art A pocket-sized Chinatown space spotlighting local and regional talent. (p84)

Best Free Entertainment

Esplanade – Theatres on the Bay Singapore's striking arts hub delivers regular free concerts and events. (p44)

Marina Bay Sands Home to Wonder Full, a twice-nightly light, laser, and water spectacular choreographed to a stirring score. (p46)

Gardens by the Bay Singapore's latest oasis comes with an after-dark sound and light show. (p28)

Little India Soak up the chaos and scents of Singapore's most colourful, hyperactive neighbourhood. (p92)

Chinatown A visceral jungle of heady temples, heritage shop-houses and wriggling market produce. (p64)

Best
Museums

Singapore is well endowed with museums, from the tiny and obscure to the ambitious and interactive. You'll find the biggest and the best in the Colonial District, where collections dive into the history, culture and art of Singapore and the continent it belongs to. Beyond them is a kooky booty of unexpected treasures, from reconstructed Chinatown slums to haunting wartime memorials.

LONELY PLANET/GETTY IMAGES ©

Museum Pass Savings

If you're visiting three or more museums during your stay, you can save money by purchasing the 3-Day Museum Pass. Costing $20 (adult) or $50 (for a family of up to five people), the pass offers unlimited admission to five National Heritage Board museums, including must-sees like the National Museum of Singapore, Asian Civilisations Museum and Peranakan Museum. The pass also covers the Singapore Art Museum. Purchase passes at any participating museum; see www.nhb.gov.sg for a complete list. Museums in Singapore usually offer significant discounts to full-time students and seniors; bring photo ID.

Lest They Forget

Singapore's WWII experience was a watershed period in its history. You'll see it covered in depth in many museums, including the National Museum of Singapore. It's also commemorated at several wartime sites, including a British fort on Sentosa, the battleground of Bukit Chandu (Opium Hill) and a former bunker in Fort Canning Park. Not surprisingly, the trauma of occupation and Singapore's tetchy postwar relations with its larger neighbours have fuelled its obsession with security today.

Best Peranakan Pickings

Peranakan Museum Explore the Peranakan world of marriage, storytelling, fashion, feasting and mourning in evocative, multimedia galleries. (p32)

Baba House Step into the private world of a wealthy Peranakan family, c 1928, at one of Singapore's most beautiful historic homes. (p72)

Katong Antique House A cluttered collection of historical objects and stories from one of Singapore's leading Peranakan historians. (p87)

Asian Civilisations Museum

Best for Art & Handicrafts

Asian Civilisations Museum A Pan-Asian treasure trove of precious decorative arts, religious artefacts, art and textiles. (p26)

National Gallery Singapore Singapore's newest cultural asset explores both 19th-century and modern regional art. (p32)

NUS Museum Permanent and temporary exhibitions of Asian ceramics and art. (p144)

Singapore Art Museum The world's largest collection of contemporary Southeast Asian art. (p32)

Gillman Barracks A rambling artillery of international galleries exhibiting revered names in modern and contemporary art. (p144)

Best for Old Singapore

National Museum of Singapore Explore centuries of Singaporean highs and lows, from exiled Sumatran princes to modern independence. (p24)

Chinatown Heritage Centre Relive the gritty, chaotic and overcrowded Chinatown of yesteryear. (p66)

Images of Singapore An interactive panorama spanning six centuries of local history. (p119)

Best for War History

Changi Museum & Chapel Sobering reflections on courage and cruelty during the WWII Japanese occupation. (p91)

Fort Siloso Slip into subterranean tunnels at this ill-fated defence fort. (p119)

Reflections at Bukit Chandu Get the lowdown on the Japanese invasion at this bite-sized museum atop Opium Hill. (p141)

Battle Box Haunting underground complex documenting the fall of Singapore. (p33)

Best
Escapes

SATYAKI CHAKRABORTI/LONELY PLANET ©

Energy meridians feeling blocked? When you have a population density of 7257 people per sq km, it's not surprising. Thankfully, Singapore has myriad ways to revive and refocus weary souls (and soles), from soothing forest canopy walks and island cycling tracks to decadent spa retreats and bargain-priced reflexology joints. Whatever your budget, slow, deep breaths are just around the corner.

City of Parks

Singapore's parks are often masterpieces of design and landscaping, from the renowned Botanic Gardens to the forests of the Southern Ridges. A huge network of park connectors enables cyclists and runners to basically circumnavigate the island without ever encountering a road. For network routes and downloadable maps, see www.nparks.com.sg.

The Rub-Down

Tight muscles have no shortage of salvation, with midrange to luxe spas in most malls and five-star hotels, and a plethora of cheaper no-frills joints in less-fashionable malls like People's Park Plaza. The latter is packed with stalls offering reflexology, shiatsu and even pools of fish that happily nibble away your dead skin cells. Rates vary from around $15 for a foot massage to over $200 for a full-day package.

Best Green Getaways

Southern Ridges Thick forest and skyline views dot this string of parks and reserves. (p140)

Singapore Botanic Gardens Catch the MRT to Singapore's manicured paradise. (p128)

Pulau Ubin Cycle your worries away on this quaint, once-upon-a-time island. (p90)

Night Safari For a different kind of nightlife. (p124)

Fort Canning Park A lush, historically rich oasis in the very heart of the city. (p33)

Best for Pampering

Remède Spa Luxe treatments at the St Regis Hotel, just off Orchard Rd. (p52)

Tomi Foot Reflexology Affordable, no-frills rubdowns in the heart of Orchard Rd (p52)

People's Park Complex The mall might be busy, but the 3rd floor will leave you purring with its bargain reflexology outlets. (p73)

Survival Guide

Survival Guide

Before You Go

When to Go

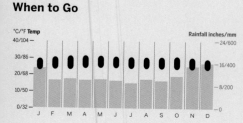

°C/°F Temp

Rainfall inches/mm

➡ Singapore is tropical and humid year-round.

➡ School holidays fall in June and July, the hottest time, so try to avoid travelling in these months if possible.

Book Your Stay

☑ **Top Tip** Midrange and top-end hotel rates are based on supply and demand, with daily fluctuations. During the Formula One night race, for example, room prices triple.

➡ Singapore is compact, with excellent public transport; your choice of location is not crucial, but it's worth picking carefully. Orchard Rd, best known for large midrange and top-end hotels, is a good choice for shopaholics. Chinatown and Tanjong Pagar are well known for smaller boutique hotels surrounded by atmospheric lanes, restaurants and nightlife. Cheap beds and a backpacker vibe define Little India, while Sentosa delivers resort-style hotels with easy access to theme parks and beaches.

➡ Book way in advance during peak periods like the Formula One Grand Prix. Even average hostels tend to fill on weekends.

➡ Hostels usually include a simple breakfast. Midrange and top-end hotels usually don't unless part of a special deal.

➡ Tipping isn't expected in hostels. At higher-end establishments, consider tipping porters $2 to $5 and housekeepers $2.

Useful Websites

Lonely Planet (www.lonelyplanet.com/singapore) Destination information and online bookings.

Your Singapore (www.yoursingapore.com) Official tourism board website.

Booking.com (www.booking.com) Online hotel search engine and booking service.

City Nomads (www.citynomads.com) A good online guide to Singapore.

Best Budget

Bunc@Radius (www.bunchostel.com) Contemporary Bunc@Radius is the coolest flashpacker hostel in Little India.

5Footway.Inn Project Boat Quay
(www.5footwayinn.com) Right on Boat Quay, this 66-room, new-school hostel is the best of four Singapore branches.

Checkers Inn (www.checkersinn.com.sg) Bright, spacious and in the heart of Little India, Checkers Inn has no shortage of fans.

Best Midrange

Wanderlust (www.wanderlusthotel.com) Idiosyncratic rooms packed with imagination, quirkiness and designer twists in intriguing Little India.

Park Regis (www.parkregissingapore.com) Attentive service, modern rooms and a pool just a stone's

throw from Chinatown and the Quays.

Holiday Inn Express (www.ihg.com) A new good-value option just a block from Orchard Rd.

Bliss Hotel (www.blisshotel.com) Budget, boutique Bliss has an enviable location right across the street from the Chinatown MRT station.

Best Top End

Fullerton Bay Hotel (www.fullertonbayhotel.com) A plush, deco-inspired number where each room comes with water views.

Parkroyal on Pickering (www.parkroyalhotels.com) A striking architectural statement, with hanging gardens and a stunning infinity pool.

Naumi (www.naumihotel.com) A slinky Colonial District hotel with commissioned artwork, playful quotes and a rooftop infinity pool.

Capella Singapore (www.capellahotels.com/singapore) An arresting melange of colonial and contemporary architecture and cascading pools on Sentosa Island.

Arriving in Singapore

From Changi Airport

This international **airport** (☎1800 542 4422; www.changiairport.com) is 20km northeast of the city centre. There are three main terminals, with a fourth terminal scheduled to open in 2017.

➡ **Bus** Public bus 36 runs from Terminals 1, 2 and 3 to Orchard Rd and the Colonial District ($1.85, one hour). Buses leave roughly every five to 15 minutes, the first departing just after 6am and the last just before 11pm.

➡ **Airport shuttle** Faster and more convenient are the airport shuttle buses (adult/child $9/6, 20 to 40 minutes) and drop passengers at any hotel, except for those on Sentosa and in Changi Village. Shuttle buses leave from Terminals 1, 2 and 3. Waiting time is up to 15 minutes during peak hours (6am to 9am and 5pm to 1am) and up to 30 minutes at all other times. Go to the Ground Transport Desk in the arrival halls.

➡ **MRT** The Mass Rapid Transit (MRT) is the best low-cost way to get into town. The station is located below Terminals 2 and 3, the fare to Orchard Rd is $2.30 and the journey takes around 40 minutes. Change trains at Tanah Merah (just cross the platform). Trains run between 5.30am (6am Sundays) and 11.18pm.

➡ **Taxi** Taxi lines at Changi are fast-moving and efficient. The fare structure is complicated, but count on spending between $18 and $38 into the city centre. The most expensive time is between 5pm and 6am, when numerous surcharges kick in. A four-seater limousine transfer service operates 24 hours a day and costs a flat $55 ($60 for a seven-seater) to anywhere on the island, plus $15 per additional stop. Enquire at the Ground Transport Desk at the airport.

Train

➡ Trains from Malaysia terminate at **Woodlands Train Checkpoint** (11 Woodlands Crossing; 🚌 170, Causeway Link from Queen St). Trains depart daily from Butterworth at 8am and Kuala Lumpur (KL) at 8.30am, 2pm and 10.30pm. Journey time is 14 hours from Butterworth and eight to 8½ hours from KL. You can book tickets either at the station or via the KTM website.

Bus

➡ Many buses arriving from Malaysia terminate at **Golden Mile Complex** (Map p97; 5001 Beach Rd), close to Kampong Glam. From Johor Bahru in Malaysia, **Causeway Link** (www.causewaylink.com.my; one-way $2.50/RM2.60; 🕐 every 15 to 30 mins, roughly 6am-11.30pm) commuter buses run regularly to various locations in Singapore, including Newton Circus, Jurong East Bus Terminal and Kranji MRT station.

Boat

There are several main ferry terminals with services from Malaysia and Indonesia.

Changi Point Ferry Terminal (☎ 6546 8518; 51 Lorong Bekukong; Ⓜ Tanah Merah then bus 2) Located 200m north of the Changi Bus Terminal.

HarbourFront Cruise & Ferry Terminal (Map p142, G5; ☎ 6513 2200; www.singaporecruise.com; Ⓜ HarbourFront)

Tanah Merah Ferry Terminal (☎ 6513 2200; www.singaporecruise.com; Ⓜ Tanah Merah then bus 35)

Getting Around

☑ **Top Tip** Singapore is the easiest city in Asia to get around. The TransitLink Guide ($2.80 from Kinokuniya book store) lists all MRT and bus routes and includes maps showing the surrounding area of all MRT stations. For online bus information, including the useful IRIS service (which offers live next-bus departure times), see www.sbstransit.com.sg or download the 'SBS Transit iris' smartphone app. For train information, see www.smrt.com.sg. There's also a consolidated website at www.publictransport.sg.

Mass Rapid Transit (MRT)

➡ Singapore's efficient metro system has five lines: the North-South (Red Line), Northeast (Purple Line), East-West (Green Line), Circle Line (Yellow) and Downtown Line (Blue). Extensions of the Downtown line (known as Downtown 2 and Downtown 3) are scheduled to open in 2016 and 2017 respectively.

➡ Trains run from 5.30am to midnight, running every two to three minutes during peak times and every five to seven minutes off-peak.

➡ Single-trip fares cost $1.40 to $2.50 (plus a $1 refundable deposit). If you're planning on multiple trips, consider purchasing the more convenient EZ-Link card or Singapore Tourist Pass.

Bus

➡ Singapore's bus service is clean, extensive and frequent, reaching every corner of the island. The two main operators are **SBS Transit** (☎1800 287 2727; www.sbstransit.com.sg) and **SMRT** (www.smrt.com.sg). Check the websites for information and routes.

➡ Fares range from $1 to $2.10 (less with an EZ-Link card). When boarding, drop the exact coins into the fare box or tap your EZ-Link card or Tourist Pass on the reader as you enter and exit.

➡ SMRT also runs late-night bus services be-

tween the city and various suburbs from 11.30pm to 2.30am on Fridays, Saturdays and the eve of public holidays. The flat rate per journey is $4.50. See the website for route details.

Taxi

➡ The 'taxi issue' is one of Singapore's big unsolvable problems and finding a taxi at certain times (peak hours, at night or when it's raining) is harder than it should be. The fare structure is complicated, but mercifully metered. Basic flagfall is $3 to $3.40, then $0.22 for every 400m. Some of the many surcharges include 50% of the metered fare from midnight to 6am,

25% of the metered fare between 6am and 9.30am Monday to Friday and 6pm to midnight daily, $5 for airport trips from 5pm to midnight Friday to Sunday ($3 at all other times), $2.30 to $8 for phone bookings and 10% for credit-card payments. You can also pay using your EZ-Link transport card. For a comprehensive list of fares and surcharges, visit www.taxisingapore.com.

➡ You can flag down a taxi any time, but in the city centre they are only at designated taxi stands.

➡ To order a taxi, call **Comfort Taxi and CityCab** (☎6552 1111), **Premier Taxis** (☎6363 6888) or **SMRT Taxis** (☎6555 8888).

Travel Passes

There are two kinds of pass for Singapore public transport that save a lot of hassle buying tickets every time you travel.

➡ Buy the **EZ-Link** card from the customer service windows at MRT stations ($12, including a $5 nonrefundable deposit). The card can also be bought at 7-Elevens for $10 (which also includes a $5 nonrefundable deposit). The card is valid on all buses and trains and can be topped up with cash or ATM cards at station ticket machines.

➡ The **Singapore Tourist Pass** (www.thesingaporetouristpass.com.sg) offers unlimited travel on trains and most buses for $10 a day, plus a refundable $10 deposit.

Essential Information

Business Hours

Opening hours can vary between individual businesses. General opening hours are as follows:

Shops 10am–6pm; malls and department stores 10am or 11am–10pm

Banks 9.30am–4.30pm Monday to Friday, some branches open at 10am and some close at 6pm or later; Saturday 9.30am to noon or later.

Restaurants noon–2pm and 6–10pm, casual restaurants, food courts and hawker centres all day

Customs

➡ It is illegal to bring tobacco unless you pay duty.

➡ The limit on alcohol is 1L each of wine, beer or spirits duty-free. Alternatively, you are allowed 2L of wine and 1L of beer, or 2L of beer and 1L of wine. You need to have been out of Singapore for more than 48 hours and to anywhere else but Malaysia.

➡ It's illegal to bring in the following items: chewing gum, firecrackers, drugs, obscene or seditious material, gun-shaped cigarette lighters, endangered species or their by-products and pirated recordings and publications.

Discounts

If you're arriving on Singapore Airlines or Silk Air, you are entitled to discounts at selected hotels, shops, restaurants and attractions by presenting your boarding pass. See www.singaporeair.com/boardingpass for details.

Electricity

230V/50Hz

➡ Plugs are of the three-pronged, square-pin type. Electricity runs at 230V and 50Hz cycles.

Emergencies

Ambulance, Fire (☏995)

Police (☏999)

Holidays

New Year's Day 1 January

Chinese New Year Three days in January/February

Good Friday March/April

Labour Day 1 May

Vesak Day June

Hari Raya Puasa July

National Day 9 August

Hari Raya Haji September

Deepavali November

Christmas Day 25 December

Money

➡ Singapore's unit of currency is the Singapore dollar.

➡ Cirrus-enabled ATM machines are widely available at malls, banks, MRT stations and commercial areas.

➡ Banks change money but currency conversion rates are better at the moneychangers. These tiny stalls can be found in most shopping centres (though not necessarily in the more modern malls). Rates for amounts over $500 can be haggled a little.

→ Credit cards are widely accepted, except at hawker centres and food courts.

Telephone

→ There are no area codes within Singapore; telephone numbers are eight digits unless you are calling toll-free (☎1800).

→ If you plan to use an unlocked phone in Singapore, it's usually cheaper to purchase a local SIM card and number for your mobile. Local SIM cards cost around $18 (including credit) from post offices, convenience stores and local Telco stores; bring your passport.

→ Roaming charges apply if using your own number, but as Singapore's two cell phone networks (GSM900 and GSM1800) make it compatible with most of the rest of the world you'll still be in business.

→ In certain areas – mostly along the coast of East Coast Park – Indonesia's signal may push into Singapore's 'airspace', so your calls will be routed through Indonesia (a potentially costly detour!)

Useful Phone Numbers

Flight Information (☎1800 542 4422)

Singapore International Dial Code (☎65)

STB Touristline (☎1800 736 2000)

Tourist Information

Singapore Tourism Board (STB; ☎1800 736 2000; www.yoursingapore.com) provides the widest range of services, including tour bookings and event ticketing. There are visitor centres at the following locations: **ION Orchard Mall** (Map p50, C3; Level 1 Concierge, ION Orchard Mall, 2 Orchard Link; ⊙10am-10pm) and **Orchard Road** (Map p50, E3; cnr Cairnhill & Orchard Rds; ⊙9.30am-10.30pm).

Travellers with Disabilities

→ Most major hotels, shopping malls and tourist attractions have good wheelchair access, but Little India and Chinatown's crowded narrow footpaths will challenge anyone with mobility, sight or hearing issues. Taxis are usually plentiful and the MRT is wheelchair-friendly.

→ The **Disabled People's Association of Singapore** (www.dpa.org.sg) has information on accessibility in the city.

Visas

→ Citizens of most countries are granted 30- or 90-day entry on arrival. Citizens of India, Myanmar, the Commonwealth of Independent States and most Middle Eastern countries must obtain a visa before arriving in Singapore. Visit www.ica.gov.sg for detailed information on entry requirements.

Tourist Buses

Singapore Airlines runs the **SIA Hop-On** (☎6338 6877; www.siahopon.com; 24hr ticket for SIA passengers adult/child $8/4, non-passengers $25/15) tourist bus, traversing the main tourist arteries every 30 minutes daily, starting at Raffles Blvd at 9am, with the last bus leaving at 7.35pm. Buy tickets from the driver.

City Hippo (☎6228 6877; www.ducktours.com.sg) offers an array of tour options round all the major sites. Twenty-four-hour tickets including a river cruise cost adult/child $33/23.

Language

The official languages of Singapore are Malay, Mandarin, Tamil and English. Malay is the national language, adopted when Singapore was part of Malaysia, but its use is mostly restricted to the Malay community.

The government's long-standing campaign to promote Mandarin, the main nondialectal Chinese language, has been very successful and increasing numbers of Singaporean Chinese now speak it at home. In this chapter we've provided Pinyin (the official system of writing Mandarin in the Roman alphabet) alongside the Mandarin script.

Tamil is the main Indian language in Singapore; others include Malayalam and Hindi. If you read our pronunciation guides for the Tamil phrases in this chapter as if they were English, you'll be understood. The stressed syllables are indicated with italics.

English is widespread and has been the official first language of instruction in schools since 1987. Travellers will have no trouble getting by with only English in Singapore.

To enhance your trip with a phrasebook, visit **lonelyplanet.com**.

Malay

Hello.	Helo.
Goodbye. (when leaving/staying)	Selamat tinggal./ Selamat jalan.
How are you?	Apa khabar?
Fine, thanks.	Khabar baik.
Please. (when asking/offering)	Tolong./ Silakan.
Thank you.	Terima kasih.
Excuse me.	Maaf.
Sorry.	Minta maaf.
Yes./No.	Ya./Tidak.
What's your name?	Siapa nama kamu?
My name is ...	Nama saya ...
Do you speak English?	Bolehkah anda berbicara Bahasa Inggeris?
I don't understand.	Saya tidak faham.
How much is it?	Berapa harganya?
Can I see the menu?	Minta senarai makanan?
Please bring the bill.	Tolong bawa bil.
Where are the toilets?	Tandas di mana?
Help!	Tolong!

Mandarin

Hello./Goodbye.	你好。/再见。	Nǐhǎo./Zàijiàn.
How are you?	你好吗？	Nǐhǎo ma?
Fine. And you?	好。你呢？	Hǎo. Nǐ ne?
Please ...	请……	Qǐng ...
Thank you.	谢谢你。	Xièxie nǐ.

Excuse me. (to get attention)
劳驾。 Láojià.

Excuse me. (to get past)
借光。 Jièguāng.

Sorry.
对不起。 Duìbùqǐ.

Yes./No.
是。/不是。 Shì./Bùshì.

What's your name?
你叫什么
名字? Nǐ jiào shénme
míngzi?

My name is ...
我叫…… Wǒ jiào ...

Do you speak English?
你会说
英文吗? Nǐ huìshuō
Yīngwén ma?

I don't understand.
我不明白。 Wǒ bù míngbái.

How much is it?
多少钱? Duōshǎo qián?

Can I see the menu?
能不能给我看
一下菜单? Néng bù néng gěiwǒ
kàngyīxià càidān?

Please bring the bill.
请给我账单。 Qǐng gěiwǒ zhàngdān.

Where are the toilets?
厕所在哪儿? Cèsuǒ zài nǎr?

Help!
救命! Jiùmìng!

Tamil

Hello.
வணக்கம். va·*nak*·kam

Goodbye.
போய வருகிறேன். po·i va·*ru*·ki·reyn

How are you?
நீங்கள் நலமா? neeng·kal na·*la*·maa

Fine, thanks. And you?
நலம், நன்றி. na·*lam nan*·dri
நீங்கள்? neeng·kal

Please.
தயவு செய்து. ta·ya·vu chey·*tu*

Thank you.
நன்றி. nan·dri

Excuse me.
தயவு செய்து. ta·ya·vu sei·*du*

Sorry.
மன்னிக்கவும். man·nik·ka·vum

Yes./No.
ஆமாம். /இல்லை. aa·maam/il·lai

What's your name?
உங்கள் பெயர் ung·kal pe·*yar*
என்ன? en·na

My name is ...
என் பெயர்... en pe·*yar* ...

Do you speak English?
நீங்கள் ஆங்கிலம் neeng·kal *aang*·ki·lam
பேசுவீர்களா? pey·chu·*veer*·ka·la

I don't understand.
எனக்கு e·*nak*·ku
விளங்கவில்லை. vi·*lang*·ka·vil·*lai*

How much is it?
இது என்ன i·*tu* en·na
விலை? vi·*lai*

I'd like the bill/menu, please.
எனக்கு தயவு e·*nak*·ku ta·ya·vu
செய்து chey·*tu*
விலைச்சீட்டு/ vi·*laich*·cheet·tu/
உணவுப்பட்டியல் u·na·*vup*·pat·ti·yal
கொடுங்கள். ko·*tung*·kal

Where are the toilets?
கழிவறைகள் ka·*zi*·va·rai·kal
எங்கே? eng·key

Help!
உதவு! u·ta·vi

Behind the Scenes

Send Us Your Feedback

We love to hear from travellers – your comments help make our books better. We read every word, and we guarantee that your feedback goes straight to the authors. Visit **lonelyplanet.com/contact** to submit your updates and suggestions.

Note: We may edit, reproduce and incorporate your comments in Lonely Planet products such as guidebooks, websites and digital products, so let us know if you don't want your comments reproduced or your name acknowledged. For a copy of our privacy policy visit lonelyplanet.com/privacy.

Our Readers

Many thanks to the travellers who used the last edition and wrote to us with helpful hints, useful advice and interesting anecdotes:

Jill Cody , Charles Hayter, Dale Holyoak, Olga Plak, Peter Yellowlees.

Cristian Bonetto's Thanks

A heartfelt thank you to Helen Burge, Alistair Cook, Felix Haubold, Chris Edwards, Jonathan Choe, Guillaume D, Mary-Ann Gardner, Sara Egan, Myles Bascao Agunit , Benjamin Milton Hampe, Michael Dean, Richie Raupe, Lim Wee Keong, and my ever-patient family.

Acknowledgments

Cover photograph: Chinese New Year celebrations, Marina Bay, Gavin Hellier/AWL

This Book

This 4th edition of Lonely Planet's *Pocket Singapore* was researched and written by Cristian Bonetto. The previous edition was also researched by Cristian and the 2nd edition was written by Joshua Samuel Brown and Mat Oakely. This guidebook was commissioned in Lonely Planet's London office, and produced by the following: **Destination Editor** Sarah Reid **Product Editor** Penny Cordner **Senior Cartographer** Julie Sheridan **Book Designer** Katherine Marsh **Assisting Editors** Victoria Harrison, Christopher Pitts **Assisting Cartographer** Rachel Imeson **Assisting Book Designer** Jennifer Mullins **Cover Researcher** Naomi Parker **Thanks to** Elin Berglund, Ryan Evans, Larissa Frost, Jouve India, Claire Naylor, Karyn Noble, Sam Tyson, Lauren Wellicome, Dora Whitaker, Tony Wheeler

Index

See also separate subindexes for:

⊗ Eating p185
🍷 Drinking p186
✪ Entertainment p187
🛍 Shopping p187

Sights 000
Map Pages **000**